"A wise and thoughtful gu

D.... Robbins
————— ....der of EarthSave and author of
MA___ .. BE FED and DIET FOR A NEW AMERICA

"This book is based on fifty years of
successful organic growing. It is an excellent
guide for the backyard gardener as well as
the commercial farmer."

Dr. Bargyla Rateaver
Organic Growing Consultant
San Diego, California

"John Harrison's book is a poem on the theme
of organic growing. I highly recommend it for all
gardeners and farmers."

Richard Bartak, C.S.R.
Deputy Minister of Agriculture
Prague, Czech Republic

"Having read John Harrison's writings on organic
growing and worked with him on the
subject of sprouting, I pray that the whole world
may follow his advice."

Dr. (Sr.) Serena
Maharaja University
Baroda, India

John Bede Harrison

Growing Food
Organically

Waterwheel Press
West Vancouver, Canada
Seattle, USA

Canadian Cataloguing in Publication Data

Harrison, John B., 1915–
  Growing food organically

  Includes index.
  ISBN 0-920641-24-5

  1. Organic gardening. 2. Organic farming.
I. Title.
SB453.5.H37 1993   635'.0484   C93-091550-X

Published in Canada by
Waterwheel Press
1352-B Marine Drive
West Vancouver, BC
Canada V7T 1B5

Published in the U.S.A. by
Waterwheel Press
620 – 1916 Pike Place
Seattle, WA 98101

Cover design by Harry Bardal
Typesetting by CompuType, Vancouver, BC
Printed and bound in Canada by Hignell Printing Ltd.

To my family, friends, and staff, and to all who love the soil.

It is my desire that all will come to know and love the soil with its vibrant multitudes of life, to admire its miracles far beyond human comprehension, and to appreciate nature's vastness and power to survive in spite of human destruction. Our knowledge of the soil in its entirety is superficial. We must regain the reverence and respect our forebears had for the soil, reverence and respect that have been almost totally lost in this era of newfound knowledge.

The Mylora Philosophy

Over fifty years' experience on our organic farm, Mylora, convinced us of the soundness of a preventive rather than a curative approach. We continuously asked ourselves "Why did the insects attack here and now?" not "What should we do about them?"

Contents

Acknowledgements

This book is the harvest of the efforts and sacrifices of our entire family. I am deeply indebted to my dear wife, Marian, and my four daughters and five sons, who have been and continue to be a constant source of encouragement and assistance through the years. I am extremely grateful to all of them: Jim, our public relations man and business specialist; Mary, who put our operation on a sound financial basis; Eileen, our nurse, who healed our hearts and wounds; Patsy, who provided us with her literary and culinary skills; Leo, who worked tirelessly in each of our many projects; David, the steady one—a true naturalist and lover of the soil; Cathy, who was always in good spirits when no one else was; Michael, our great organizer and diplomat; and Steve, our Jack-of-all-trades and our affectionate youngest.

They are our children forever. Marian always played to the full her strong, supportive role, and with her radiant smile she smoothed the rough bumps along life's road. For many years she carried a heavy burden, nurturing the children with patience, encouragement, and understanding, and playing a vital role in the business by managing our sales staff at the roadside stand where we sold our produce. Because of Marian, each one of the staff came to feel a part of our family, reflecting the consideration and loyalty she inspired.

The seeds of thought for writing a book about organic growing were sown as I read *Pleasant Valley* by Louis Bromfield. The book was a gift from my wife, and it was she who helped me to harvest the ripened crop of experience. Betty O'Neil's faith and way with words provided a welcome green thumb for presenting the crop.

My gratitude also goes to my sister, Mary Harrison, for her great public relations work and her encouragement. Through her community work, Mary has made wide connections and has introduced me to many who share the Mylora philosophy. My loyal and devoted staff, particularly Susi Vere, have also been a great help to me, and when I needed scientific information, Miriam Schoenfeld was ever ready with her vast store of knowledge. Among my many good friends in the departments of agriculture, Gordon Thorpe and John Webster have generously shared their wisdom with me.

The publication of this book is also due in no small measure to the persistence of Bargyla Rateaver, an organic farm consultant in California, and, closer to home, to one of my former organic farming students, Russell Precious. It was he who put me in touch with my publisher, Gordon Soules. I discovered that Gordon was one of our former good customers who, throughout the years, regularly drove a long way from his home to purchase our organically grown food to nourish his family.

My deep appreciation goes to Irene Frith, former Richmond Councillor, who realized that our organic family farming business was dangerously jeopardized by two different arms of government: one department destroyed the wholeness of the farm, bisecting it with a freeway and providing no compensation, and the marketing board refused to renew our permission to sell our specially grown, organic food, thus destroying the market we had spent many years developing. Irene assisted us through the proper civic channels and so helped us to change the direction of our efforts. My gratitude also goes to my former business partners, Jack Reykdal and Al Austin, who helped in so many ways.

I am grateful for the dependable staying power, encouragement, and skill of Florence Newmark. Many other friends and associates have constantly encouraged me on that lonely road that one who thinks differently is compelled to travel. Without realizing it, these people gave their support in words and deeds—even a smile was like an oasis in the desert: Fr. J. Murray Abraham, S.J., Darjeeling, India; Sr. Alcantara, Uganda; Barbara Anderson; Claude Aubert, France; Jean Baker; Lady Eve Balfour, London, England; Ing. Richard Bartak, CSc Deputy Minister of Agriculture, Prague, Czechoslovakia; Patricia Battle; Hilda Beastall; Dennis Becker; Ella Berznick; Katie Bissett; Gilbert Blair; Dr. Joseph Boucher; Lois Boyce; Pat Burns; Mickey Carlton; Christopher Chapman; Spencer Cheshire; Frances Clark; Mary Cleveland; Stuart Clugston; Duncan Cumming; Alan Daniels; John Davies; Maria and Frank Dietl; Dr. James Douglas; Alan Eadie; Georgiana Evans; Marshal Finlayson; Dr. Patrick Finney, U.S.A.; Fr. Thomas Fitzpatrick, S.J., Ethiopia; Frank Ford, U.S.A.; Sr. Millicent Francis, Rome, Italy; Dr. Patricia Fulton; Br. Guy Gartland; Drew Gillies, N.F.B.; Edward Gilmore; Lewis and Rosemary Glavina; Jerome Goldstein, U.S.A.; Prof. Tara Gopaldas, Baroda, India; Margaret T. Gourlay; Birdie Gray; John Hall, Q.C.; Marianne Hamilton; Phyllis Hanes; Sheila Harrington; Christie Harris; Dr. Geoffrey Hawtin, I.D.R.C.; Prof. Stuart Hill; Margaret Hollingsworth; Ida Honoroff, U.S.A.; Bob Hunter; Roy Jacques; Sr. Jerome; Thelma Johnston; Nathan Keats; Dr. Louis Kervran, Paris, France; Anne Kloppenborg; Karol Koncko, Bratislava, Czechoslovakia; Jim Langan; Joanne Leach; Ivan Lipovsky; Dr. Wilbald Lorri, Dar es Salaam, Tanzania; Shirley Lynn; Thelma McAdam;

Sr. Rosemary McCaffrey, Missionary Sisters of Africa; Fr. Thomas McGivern, S.J., Lusaka, Zambia; Rick McGrath; Br. Gerrard McHugh, Rome, Italy; Br. Ron McKenzie; Laureen McMahon; Roderick C. Macrae, P. Eng.; John Madeley, London, England; Margaret Mahoney; Dr. Fred Miller, U.S.A.; Theo and Michael J. Miller; Jeanine Mitchell; Desmond and Elizabeth Montague; Betty Morales, U.S.A.; Ronald Morgan; Edward Moxey; Norma Myers; Dr. Joe Nichols, U.S.A.; Eric Nicol; Peggy O'Connell; Betty O'Neil; Dee Palmer, B.B.C., London, England; Lorne Parton; Dennis Peterson; Dr. Dan Phelps; Dr. Bargyla Rateaver, U.S.A.; Maurie Redman; Mary Richardt; Dr. Roger Rogers; Dorothy Romalis; Evelyn Root; Leslie J. Ross; John Sawatsky; Miriam Schoenfeld; Reindeer Schuitema; Sr. Serena, Baroda, India; the Rt. Hon. the Viscount John Sidmouth, Wilts., England; Eve Smith; Arran Stephens; David Stickland, London, England; Roland Syens; Robert Tait; David Terry; Peter Thornton; John Tobe; Beatrice Trum-Hunter; Don Tuline; Louis Van Der Gracht; William Warner; Jack Webster; Dr. Anne Wigmore, U.S.A.; John Woodley, South Africa; Dr. Gerry Wright; George Zambosky, Bratislava, Czechoslovakia; Kareen Zebroff.

Several editors brought their skills to this book. Nancy Flight, Yvonne Van Ruskenveld, Joanne Broatch, and Gudrun Will have all been wonderful. Through it all, Joy Woodsworth was the efficient typesetter. Artist Harry Bardal did a magnificent job of the book design and illustrations. Finally, when difficulties arose, and we could no longer agree, there was always Gordon's wife, Christine, in the wings; we all respected her judgement. Thank you all again. I apologize for any names I may have accidentally omitted, or any incorrect or missing titles.

It was a tremendous help that we all shared the bond of concern about the earth and the abuse it has been enduring and that we have accepted our responsibility to care for this earth and to hand on to future generations a truly fertile soil. My heartfelt gratitude goes to all those thoughtful persons near and far who have been concerned directly or indirectly with the care of our earth and all its inhabitants. I am especially grateful to those brave professional people who have risked their future by speaking out about the threat of chemical dependency. I am grateful too to the owners of health food stores and allied businesses who have risked their savings; to their employees who, for the good cause, have accepted less than the usual wages; to the publishers, authors, and members of the media who so helpfully spread the word far and wide— all doing the best they could in their own ways; and to all organic farmers, who are really the fighters on the front line.

Chapter One
A Personal Story

It is the Earth, like a kind mother, receives us at our birth, and sustains us when born. It is this alone, of all the elements around us, that is never found an enemy to man. The body of waters deluge him with rains, oppress him with hail and drown him with inundations; the air rushes in storms, prepares the tempest, or lights up the volcano; but the Earth, gentle and indulgent, ever subservient to the wants of man, spreads his walks with flowers and his table with plenty. Returns with interest every good committed to her care and though she produces the poison, she still supplies the antidote. Though constantly teased the more to furnish the luxuries of man than his necessities, yet even to the last she continues her kind indulgence and when life is over she piously hides his remains in her bosom.

Pliny

This book is a celebration of the miracle of the soil, with its teeming life and its ability to nourish humankind. It is a call to examine the role of the soil in building up our natural resources, and it offers proof that organic growing is the only real solution to the mounting agricultural pollution that threatens the earth.

Over half a century of organic growing has convinced me of the soundness, stability and permanence of organic culture. As a boy growing up in Sydney, Australia, I spent my summer holidays in the sheep-raising country of New South Wales, where my grandfather had a sheep station, or ranch, called Mylora (an aboriginal word meaning "deep pool"). Here I spent my time riding horses, mustering the sheep for shearing, branding and dipping, and doing chores detested by all small boys of my generation—cutting wood, pumping water and carrying things from one place to another. I remember well the chill of early morning, the smell of the dust stirred up by the hooves of the sheep and the excited bark of the sheep dogs as they herded wanderers back to the flock.

After leaving school, I decided to become a farmer and so went to work at Mylora. Several months of work there convinced me that I needed formal training, so I took a two-year course at the State Agricultural Experimental Station at Wagga Wagga in Australia. Many phases of agriculture were included in this valuable course—the cultivation and growing of grains, fruits, vegetables and fodder; dairying; and the care and finishing of pigs, beef cattle and poultry. I then qualified as a jackeroo, an apprentice farmer who lives on the station of the owner as a member of his family.

My first job as a jackeroo was on a 3,000-acre (1200-hectare) sheep station in the Snowy River district in New South Wales. Then I worked in the outback of the western plains of New South Wales in a totally different milieu. That station was one of the largest in the state— extending over an area of 850,000 acres (340 000 hectares) in the hot, dry country. It was 50 miles (80 kilometres) from the nearest town.

The dryness of those western plains introduced many complicated factors, which occupied most of my working life at the station. Thirsty sheep often walked long distances following the scent of water, only to find their waterhole dried up. They would huddle together to await death unless they were rescued and transported to other water supplies. When the rains did come after prolonged dry spells, they were too heavy for the parched soil to absorb. The water would spread out over the flat ground, creating wide, shallow watercourses in the lowland. The sheep, by nature unwilling to walk through even very shallow water, just stood still waiting to be rescued, thus necessitating search-and-rescue efforts by all hands, including the cook.

Although the rains provided welcome relief from the months of dryness and dust, they too brought problems. The growth of fresh, green grass with its laxative effect caused digestive upsets in the flocks, usually leading to an outbreak of diarrhea. These scours, combined with the normal body excreta, attracted blowflies, which laid their eggs in the soiled wool of the sheep. As the maggots hatched, they caused great distress to the sheep, and the soiled wool had to be clipped prematurely to offer relief and destroy the maggots. Although I have been accused of seeing Mother Nature through an optimistic haze, I became well acquainted with the harsher moods of that capricious being as a result of such experiences.

Wanting to begin farming my own land, I returned to my family, who had moved to Canada. I then acquired an 80-acre (32-hectare) piece of land in British Columbia on Lulu Island. I named my farm Mylora.

Lulu Island was so named by a nineteenth-century captain of one of the coastal steamers that plied the waters between Vancouver and San Francisco, in honor of one of the favored entertainers of the era. Today it is called Richmond.

Richmond is situated south of Vancouver. The climate is mild, with winter temperatures that seldom plunge to 32°F (0°C); snowfall is minimal, with no snowfall at all some winters. The entire island is below high-tide levels, and municipal pumps provide drainage and give protection against high tides and the occasional flooding by the Fraser River, which surrounds the island. Yearly rainfall averages about 35 inches (89 centimetres), with rain mainly in the fall and winter months. Summer temperatures rarely exceed 80°F (27°C) but, as in the winters, the humidity level is relatively high and can be enervating to those who are not used to such a climate.

The central part of the island evolved over the centuries into a peat bog, and harvesting of this peat was once an important industry. Blueberries and cranberries are now grown in areas from which the top layer of peat has been removed. From the edges of the bog to the outer part of the island, the soil is a fine clay, which at the fringe of the island is mixed with sand. Mylora itself is situated between the fringe area and the peat bog.

The eventful day that I took possession of my property was October 23, 1938. The farm had been operating as a dairy farm producing milk for the Vancouver market, and I continued this operation while becoming acquainted with local conditions. Besides the routine agricultural chores associated with the dairy business, I also grew oats, hay, corn for silage and a few staple food products such as potatoes. Later my program included fattening beef cattle as well as producing clover seed, sugar beet seed and turnip seed.

Marriage and family responsibilities made the production of a higher return a pressing necessity, and accordingly I planted my first commercial crop of strawberries in 1947. This led to the establishment of our roadside marketing stand, which we maintained for many years.

At the time we were celebrating the bumper strawberry crop and the success of the new marketing venture, we were unaware that a fungus disease of strawberries called Red Stele was to make its appearance a few years later and gradually spread throughout all our fields. When it came, many years passed before were we able to produce a strawberry crop equal to that first fine harvest of strawberries.

That first year of commercial farming was also memorable because it marked the beginning of my conversion to organic growing. I had read Louis Bromfield's *Pleasant Valley* and later *Malabar Farm,* both of which documented the author's experiences and growing faith in organic farming techniques. Following this delightful introduction, I pursued the subject in all the books I could find. There were all too few. I was convinced by the reasoning of the authors of these books that organic principles were the only sound, natural foundations for agriculture because they could be continued indefinitely with better results season after season. This was in marked contrast to what I had seen of intensive chemical farming, where varieties of food plants would no longer grow satisfactorily and once-rich fields were deteriorating. What Bromfield described was very different from what I had experienced up to that time.

Converting my farm to an organic one was not only a long and difficult process but a lonely one as well. There was no one I could turn to for advice. My bright beacons of hope were the successes of individuals scattered far and wide, reported in the few periodicals devoted to organic farming.

People operating outside the generally accepted and established routines soon learn that the luxury of complaining and the salve of sympathy over failures are not usually extended to them by their peers. My neighbors and fellow farmers found little ground for common discussion with me, even though our pest problems were sometimes similar. Their suggestions usually involved using a newer chemical or increasing the dosage of an old one, while I still pondered over what soil or drainage adjustments should be made. My problem could have any number of causes, such as the time of seeding, the vagaries of the weather or the continuous monoculture practiced on the land before I farmed it. I was firmly convinced that the key to solving all such problems lay in the environment and, particularly, in a healthy living soil.

Experiments at Mylora were like final examinations at school. If the project was a failure, then another year or season had to elapse before conditions were such that we could try again with whatever changes seemed appropriate. Insects and disease destroyed crops completely or partially while we were building up the soil. Our goal was to develop within the soil a harmonious, thriving population of organisms and microorganisms. These would then be actively involved in devouring waste organic matter and converting it into the ideal soil necessary to nourish the hungry plant roots.

While we were building up the soil, we also had much to learn about the other environmental requirements of each of the different plants we wished to grow. Was it too hot for lettuce? Too cold for tomatoes? Too wet for strawberries? Too dry for peas? Too early for beans? Too late for onions? There were always lots of questions to be answered at Mylora, and the years that followed my 1947 decision to adopt organic farming techniques provided a continual learning experience.

About two years ago, I received a letter from a Czech citizen named Karol Koncko, who wrote that "only a miracle can save our people's health and this miracle is organic growing that you wrote about in your book."

He had bought a copy of *Good Food Naturally,* the title of the first edition of this book, in London about twenty years earlier and had been impressed by the principles, the reasoning and the practical advice in it. The Communist government had refused to have the book published in Czechoslovakia because the book states most explicitly that no chemicals are to be used in agriculture. The government at that time insisted that farmers use chemicals and forbade the use of manure. Farmers were forbidden even to talk about organic farming. In spite of the ban, Karol had translated the book and printed it with a hand press. For eighteen years, until the fall of Communism, he distributed it underground in five- and ten-copy lots at great personal risk. In his letter, he explained that Czechoslovakia was one of the most environmentally damaged countries in Europe, that life expectancy was down, that the birthrate was alarmingly low and that infant mortality was up. Czech food was so polluted that it was unsuitable for the world market. Karol asked to buy the rights to publish the book in his country, and he wanted to send some students to our farm in Canada for instruction in organic growing. By then, however, we had already been retired from farming for some time, so I offered instead to go to Czechoslovakia.

Jim, my oldest son; Karol, our constant companion and translator; and I travelled about 600 miles (965 kilometres), giving lectures throughout the farming country of Slovakia. While we were there, we attended a conference on organic growing sponsored by Agrosana, an organization whose aim is to establish organic growing in Czechoslovakia. We donated the royalties from the Czechoslovakian edition of *Good Food Naturally* to the Czech people for ten years. We also donated all the tapes, slides and videos used during our lecture tour. During this lecture trip, at a resort called Horna Marikova, Agrosana inaugurated the Harrison Foundation for Organic Farming in Czechoslovakia to honor and thank us for our help. It was a highly emotional moment for all of us—for students, for the officials, for Jim and for me. We became close friends, sharing so many experiences, that the thought of parting seemed to draw us even closer together. The sad day eventually arrived. We had been there about twelve days, covering a great deal of the country and speaking to many wonderful people.

One year later, I returned to Czechoslovakia with another son, David, to celebrate the release of twenty thousand copies of the Czechoslovakian edition of *Good Food Naturally*. In Revuca, Karol's home town, I addressed students as well as a small group of farmers interested in advancing their knowledge of organic gardening. They asked me about their potatoes—a most important staple food for them all. The government had allotted each household a garden space of about one-tenth of an acre (0.04 hectare), situated a short distance beyond the housing subdivision where each house had its own garden a little larger than the house itself. The general complaint was that the potato crop was decreasing each year. Blight had been attacking the plants earlier every year for the last six years. As a result, they were not getting enough potatoes for their own families.

On inquiring about their agricultural methods, I discovered that in the spring they worked up the soil, planted the potato seeds, cultivated them, cleaned out the weeds, harvested the potatoes and left the field bare, with no vegetation growing on it for all the months between harvesting and planting. That is a long period of time to allow the soil to be exposed to the destructive force of harsh weather. The people told me that they were doing just as the government did, but they did not realize that the government had money for fertilizer and lots of land, so it could use fresh fields and rest some land so that it could recover. The Czech people did not have this opportunity.

The people couldn't get manure, since none was available. They had no money to buy seed for green manure crops to improve the soil. In the meantime, the crops were deteriorating. The soil was suffering more and more from neglect and impoverishment. My only suggestion to them was to ask the government for more land so that they could leave the area they were using alone and allow it to refurbish itself, which it will do in time. I never did find out the response to this suggestion.

In contrast, the kitchen gardens in people's back yards were all small but vigorous and beautiful, because people were prevented by circumstances beyond their control from committing the errors of modern agriculture. These were truly organic gardens.

Since there was only a small area, people had to grow as wide a variety of vegetables as possible, and this forced them to plant polyculturally. As soon as some plants were being harvested, still others would replace them. There was no bare, uncovered soil, no machinery and therefore no soil compaction. Fortunately, the farmers could afford neither chemical sprays nor fertilizers. Most of them had a few chickens, a pig or two, some rabbits. Their manure was carefully placed on the garden, and flowers and vegetables grew in sweet profusion.

On this trip I also carried out numerous TV, radio and newspaper inteviews and had several speaking engagements in Bratislava and lectured at an agricultural college on a large organic farm. The entire school of three hundred students attended my lectures with keen interest. They were eager and asked many probing questions. I saw beautiful, organically grown crops of carrots and cabbage with no insect damage. Since it was mid-September, vegetables in some fields were being harvested. Many other fields were being prepared for seeding winter crops to protect the soil from seasonal damage.

During those lectures in Czechoslovakia, I spoke of ideas about organic growing that have come to mind since the publication of *Good Food Naturally*. These ideas have developed and matured in the reflective time after my years of active farming.

During both of the journeys to Czechoslovakia, Karol, his wife Anna, and their daughter Pat were the perfect hosts to my sons and myself. Their love, affection and consideration was without equal. Karol arranged for all the talks I gave and introduced me to concerned people who could understand English. Everything went off with clockwork precision. As we moved around the country, they introduced us to many of their friends, who were most gracious and welcomed us into their homes. Karol was our translator, our guide, our manager, our P.R. man, and our diplomat. I only hope that one day I may repay them for their many acts of kindness to all of us.

In recent years, I have become quite involved in promoting sprouting as a way of improving nutrition in developing countries. Dr. (Sr.) Serena, of Baroda, India, writes: "Ever since 1987, Mr. Harrison and I have been sharing our work on sprouting. I also appreciate greatly the work he has done in the area of organic farming. Having read John Harrison's writings on organic growing and worked with him on the subject of sprouting, I pray that the whole world may follow his advice."

Chapter Two
Why Organic Growing?

Ill fares the land, to hast'ning ills a prey,
Where wealth accumulates, and men decay.

Oliver Goldsmith

Oliver Goldsmith wrote these words over two hundred years ago, in the elegaic poem "The Deserted Village." Yet his words ring true today as the huge multinationals swallow up their smaller and weaker competition until they have complete control. It is chastening to read these prophetic words about what may soon become "the deserted earth." Before it is too late we must reclaim the land, purify the air and waterways, and replace materialism with a genuine reverence for life in all its forms. If we fail, future generations will be denied good physical and mental health, perhaps even life itself. Surely there is a social obligation for each of us to agitate, to plan and to work towards halting the poisoning, befouling and desecrating of the most basic life-giving elements of soil, air and water on this, our planet.

How have we been brought to this desperate condition? In the letter of dedication of his poem to Sir Joshua Reynolds, Goldsmith reiterates his belief that the price of luxury is the destruction of whole classes of society. Can we deny his claim? His concern was for the passing of the agricultural labouring class in England. Our concern must be for all children of all classes, of all the countries of the world. It must be for the preservation of the air, the water and the earth itself.

Society generally considers food an article of commerce, no more important than any other article, even less important than the fickle dollar that purchases it. This idea must be changed and food returned to its rightful position in society. Without it, absolutely everything else is superfluous.

For orthodox or chemical growers, financial return is paramount. As a result, they are primarily concerned with the appearance and the quantity of the food they grow. What really *should* be the most important factor—the nourishment provided by the food—is of lesser importance.

Since the profit motive outweighs all others under our present economic system, society is faced with a dilemma: should we continue to grow food for profit while the product deteriorates in nutritive value? Or could we change our priorities and grow food for the purpose of nourishing people properly? Such a change would demand that we all see the proper relationship between food and money, appearance and pollution, quality and quantity. The problem is that orthodox (or chemical) growers are trying to marry off the immutable principles of biology to the fickle whims of economics. Such a marriage will not work. It will be fruitless.

In their desire to reap profits, chemical farmers tend to overlook and generally denigrate the role of the natural forces of life. Instead, they attempt to impose their will on nature—for example, by using synthetic chemicals on their crops.

For some years, chemical farmers were under few restrictions on the quantity or types of chemicals that they used to grow food. In the past, growers were advised by government publications that certain chemicals were not to be used on crops that were to be fed to beef cattle or milk cows. Yet in these very same publications, two such chemicals, DDT and chlordane, were listed among those recommended for use in growing human food. Fortunately, authorities have now seen the light and imposed tighter restrictions on their use.

Scientists still know very little about the chemical and biological changes that nature produces in the soil. They know even less about the long-term effects of changes in the soil, and ultimately the environment, that are brought about by the addition of chemicals. Nevertheless, not only are farmers permitted to use such possibly dangerous materials, they are encouraged to use them. Furthermore, the labels on the packages of those chemicals seldom, if ever, tell the user these facts about the chemicals:

1. They may not wash out of the soil or break down into more harmless substances quickly.
2. They may remain in the soil indefinitely.
3. Each successive application can gradually increase the concentration of the chemical in the soil.
4. They may produce ill effects in areas far removed from where they are applied.
5. They may affect subsequent crops.
6. They may change the character of the soil itself.
7. They affect the water in streams and rivers, as well as the soil and the atmosphere.

Orthodox farmers believe that they must destroy pests that threaten to damage crops, since their yields may be reduced. In destroying pests, they frequently adopt a blitzkrieg strategy of total destruction. The deadly chemicals they use may be effective for a few seasons, but the pests eventually develop an immunity to them, and the resulting biological imbalance becomes a major problem.

Two common products of conventional farming procedures are major causes of agricultural pollution. One is residue from chemical fertilizer and pesticides, which is carried from the soil to adjacent water. The other is manure from careless livestock operations, which mixes with rain and natural drainage and seeps into the waterway. These seepages cause marine vegetation to grow more abundantly, and this proliferating growth uses up increasing amounts of oxygen. The water eventually becomes too oxygen-poor to support fish life. Pesticides finding their way into local waterways pollute as well, but their lethal effects extend into the atmosphere, far beyond the area of original use. Even penguins in the polar regions have been found to have pesticides in their body tissue. The full impact of such materials on the environment is still unknown. Yet their use is widespread, and demand for them increases yearly.

Tax-supported research and laboratory facilities in our universities and in provincial and federal departments of agriculture have become partners with industry in testing the safety and efficacy of these chemicals. I believe that those who profit by the sales of such materials should pay all the costs of independent testing. They should also bear the responsibility for the ecological disasters too often produced by their use.

The marriage of science and agriculture has melded admirably with the profit system and seems perfectly acceptable, providing that it does not affect the health of the public. Unfortunately, agricultural practices that disregard the laws of nature do affect the physical health of the public and the economic health of the farmer.

In Canada, the potential for growing food is enormous, and we produce far more than we need. Some of this food is sold or given to other countries, it is true, but enormous quantities are stored by farmers waiting for markets.

The knowledge that such quantities of food exist is a reassuring thought, easily dispelling the specter of famine from our minds. However, this comforting insurance against national hunger is a heavy and unfair financial burden forced on individual farmers. For example, farmers must pay the cost of storage as well as suffer loss by shrinkage of the food while it is stored.

It is now recognized that even a small surplus over the market requirements, particularly of perishable crops, can depress the price for the entire crop. Being dependent on nature, farmers never know how great or how small their harvest will be or how much they will have available for sale the next year. It is here that the economics of food products, especially perishables, differs greatly from that of nonfood products; when the crops are bountiful the price drops, not just on the surplus amount, but on the entire crop, whereas the cost of producing the crop remains stable. Manufacturers can control the quantity of goods they produce to suit market fluctuations. Should they miscalculate and be unable to sell all the goods they have produced in their regular markets, they can usually find outlets for the surplus goods at lower prices in different areas. Unlike the price of farmers' crops, this lower price applies only to the goods they could not sell on their regular markets and does not affect the price of the entire inventory.

Farm surpluses are normal occurrences, but the unpredictability of forecasting them and the cost of storing them make the farmers' economic position precarious. The rising labor and equipment costs, the farmers' determination to keep their farms, their sole source of income, and these surpluses all play a part in forcing farmers to destroy the source of their livelihood. They must take more and more from the soil with each succeeding crop and, in the end, destroy the very piece of land that has been supporting them.

Chemicals seemed to be a godsend to farmers on this treadmill of uncertainty, promising a cheaper means to produce crops. Farmers had no reason to be suspicious of them, since these chemicals were offered by highly trained scientists and approved by government agencies. When a new chemical was introduced, the farmers who first used it had the financial advantage of relatively low costs and increased yield. Once the chemical was widely used and the lower cost accepted, however, the price of the entire crop dropped. In their eagerness to recapture costs and sell their perishable produce, farmers competed by lowering prices. Farmers were then back on the treadmill with the same financial pressure as before. They may have gained a reprieve in the battle to keep their land, but if the land is being depleted and poisoned as well, it is a hollow victory. The consumer buys food at lower prices but pays the cost in accepting less nourishing food and suffering adverse long-term effects caused by chemicals.

Another stopgap development in economic farm problems seems, at first glance, to offer some relief to retiring farmers. This is the demand for farmland by speculative investors who have no interest in farming. They compete with one another and pay farmers an inflated price for their land. This inflated and artificial price is completely disproportionate to the amount of farm income the land can produce. Farmers wishing to expand their operations cannot afford to buy such land at the inflated price. They can afford only to rent it, becoming tenant farmers.

Tenant farmers, without the security and stability of long-term leases, do not have the same interest in maintaining the fertility of the soil that they would have as owners. They become much more interested in obtaining all the profit they can immediately, for they may be unable to rent that piece of land again the next year. Farmers who were once thrifty stewards of their land are then forced to become exploiters, and everyone loses in the long run. Economics forces more and more farmers off the land, and a greater and still greater proportion of farm land is rented and exploited. The depleted and poisoned soil then becomes a serious issue of national importance.

If society had paid more attention and adopted the practice and principles of agriculture laid down by Sir Albert Howard at the beginning of our century, the latter part of this century might have been quite different. As a British agricultural officer stationed in India, he was commissioned by his government to salvage the tea industry. Britain was feeling the economic loss caused by the decline in profits from the tea plantations. Sir Albert Howard demonstrated the intimate relationship and interdependency between the health of the soil, the health of the plants growing on that soil and the health of the animals who consumed the plants. He further demonstrated the principles of natural plant growth, which are known today as the basis of organic or natural growing. Howard documented his findings and presented them to the Royal Geographic Society. Subsequently his methods were adopted in parts of the English-speaking world by various determined individuals, almost always in the face of strong opposition. Sir Albert Howard is indeed the father of organic growing.

Hoof and mouth disease was rampant among the cattle in India at that time, and Howard's work oxen were also infected. Not only did he cure them, but he also maintained the resistance of his herd to this disease by applying his organic principles when growing their fodder. Fear of this virulent disease has caused many prime cattle in Canada to be slaughtered in attempts to stop its spread. As yet, I know of no experiments aimed at controlling it by attending to the organic condition of the soil or other environmental factors.

It is strange that Howard's findings seemed to be either unread or ignored. However, the Soil Association, which he founded in England, is attracting many new supporters of its principles, and it has even enjoyed some financial encouragement from the British government.

Sir Robert McCarrison, a British medical officer in India at the same time as Howard, not only corroborated Howard's work but pursued the subject through further experimentation and observation.

McCarrison visited many tribes throughout India and was greatly impressed by the Hunzas, a people living in a then almost inaccessible area. The Hunzas evolved an excellent agricultural technique based on their observations of nature's way. Their vibrant health, their remarkably pleasant dispositions and the large number of active, elderly people were a striking contrast to other inhabitants of that vast country and even to those of our own.

McCarrison was one of the few scientists to properly document the relationship between the health of the soil and the health of the plant, health that is transferred to the animal consumer and finally to humans. Unfortunately, his ideas were overshadowed by the exciting medical discoveries of sulfa drugs at the beginning of World War II and later by the even more exciting discovery of antibiotics. Mass production made these drugs readily available to the public. But such products were aimed at treatment, whereas McCarrison's ideas were concerned with prevention. Prevention is neither as profitable nor as dramatic as cure, so it did not arouse public attention, even though it is certainly less painful and less expensive. Both Howard's and McCarrison's work clearly showed that if a living organism has an adequate diet and correct living conditions, it will thrive. Conversely, if some of the necessary ingredients are lacking, the organism will suffer and its organs degenerate.

The studies by Howard and McCarrison of degenerative diseases in plants, animals and people added greatly to our sparse knowledge of nutrition. But the growth of knowledge about the relationship between good nutrition and good health and well-being has not kept pace with the development of agricultural chemicals. The reason for this lag is that much money can be made from the sale of chemicals, but there will be no immediate financial benefit to the farmer until the majority of the public demands unpoisoned, nutritious food. There is far more money to be made in selling vitamins to supplement food that has less than its full nutritional value.

Nutritious food has everything to do with personal health. It is thus an urgent necessity to meld the two great sciences of nutrition and agriculture and direct them towards a common goal: a healthy, happy, productive person.

If the melding of these sciences was important in McCarrison's and Howard's time, it is even more important now. Although North Americans like to think of themselves as the healthiest people in the world, evidence has shown that this is far from true. When the United States was recruiting men to fight the Korean War, Selective Service figures revealed that about 50 percent of the men recruited were unfit for service on either mental or physical grounds. In postmortem examinations of 300 men killed in combat, it was found that 80 percent of them showed early disease of the heart or arteries, although their average age was only 22. Conversely, few Koreans showed any evidence of these degenerative diseases. One report from the American Heart Association about that time states that among adults 20 years of age and older, 27 million Americans are living with some form of cardiovascular illness. Although it is fashionable to blame the stress and pace of modern life for the steady rise in heart disease and other degenerative diseases, it seems more likely that a lifetime of poor nutrition could be responsible for the weakened tissue that cannot resist such diseases for long.

When we try to find what constitutes good, bad or indifferent food, we are exploring unknown territory. Scientists can determine if certain components are lacking or if some exceed the estimated average amount. This knowledge is purely relative, however, because the optimum quantity of nutritional components in any food is still unknown. Biological components pose an even more difficult question.

Nowhere was this so clearly made evident as in the furor over dry cereals thirty years ago. The U.S. Food and Drug Administration condemned the dry cereal industry for foisting products with little or no nutritional value on an unsuspecting public. The long lists of vitamins, minerals, percentages and daily requirements listed on the packages and couched in proper scientific terminology were too impressive to be disbelieved. Yet a closer examination of the wording revealed the emptiness of the claims: some neglected to mention that the nutritional values included milk that had to be added to the serving. This manipulation of the public is reprehensible because it seeks to make a profit out of a gradually growing concern for health. We must have more exact information about our nutritional needs. We must have meaningful standards of food quality.

How much less worrisome this would be if all food were organically or naturally grown and therefore nutritionally adequate.

Since nature is the prime agriculturist, organic growers copy nature's ways as closely as possible. Organic agriculture is based on nature's own system of polyculture, the growing of a mixture of plants in one area. Modern, non-organic farming, however, is based on monoculture, the planting of only one kind of plant in an area. Since such plants are seeded simultaneously and grow at the same rate, they will touch one another as they increase in size. Therefore, any adversity affecting one plant easily spreads throughout the entire plantation. Worst of all, these plants grow in soil polluted with their own excreta. Mono-culturally grown plants have no natural controls, such as adequate distance from one another, different strengths and weaknesses, and varying stages of maturity. Insects and disease easily sweep through such areas. It is no wonder that famine and other disasters strike in areas of large, monoculturally grown crops.

Whereas modern farming seeks to control pests, organic agriculture works to prevent unbalanced growing conditions that invite pests in the first place. Organic growing ensures that a plant has built-in protection against its natural enemies, which only attack a plant already unfit to reproduce or nourish higher forms of life.

Our ancestors used organic agriculture until the advent and subsequent abuse of agricultural chemistry. This abuse means that the chemically grown food we buy is polluted, and polluted food pollutes our bodies.

The organic grower produces food to nourish people. In organic agriculture, all life forms—including soil microorganisms, insects, bees and birds—receive as much consideration as the end consumers, human beings. Organic growers realize that humans depend on a great hierarchy of less-complex life forms for food.

Poets, philosophers and theologians through the ages have been convinced that all life forms together constitute one indivisible entity and that damage to any one part is damage to every part. To the organic grower, the complete cycle of life constitutes the entity, a weakness in any part of which undermines the strength of the entire cycle.

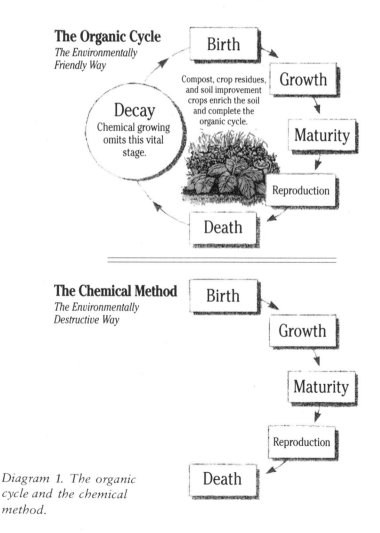

Diagram 1. The organic cycle and the chemical method.

The cycle of life consists of birth, growth, maturity, reproduction, death and decay. Decay, being the last link, is joined again to the first, birth or rebirth, completing the cycle that is absolutely necessary for continued life on this earth. In nature, the cycle of life remains intact.

In celebrating the first part of the cycle, the birth of new life, we often lose sight of the fundamental importance of the last part, decay. The products of decay are designed by nature to nourish organisms in the soil. Such organisms provide food for plants growing in this soil. They in turn nourish animals, continuing the cycle naturally and without interruption down through the millennia. This cycle remained closed and functioned perfectly up until the time of the Industrial Revolution in England, when food became a more important article of commerce.

The cycle has now been broken at one vital link, the link of decay. We no longer see the importance of replenishing the soil with natural life-giving material. Instead, we relegate such material to garbage cans, landfills and incinerators; even worse, we then try to "enrich" the soil with chemicals, which eventually destroy its natural vitality. The plants grown in this polluted and dying soil cannot possibly absorb and pass on the full range of nutrients that we require to nourish ourselves properly. Since no one knows what all those nutrients are, we must take great care not to accidentally eliminate even one of them because that one might be of vital importance.

A dying soil lacks not only nutrients but also humus, one of the main ingredients that hold the soil particles together. Without humus, soil has no structure: the particles become like dust or fine sand and are extremely vulnerable to winds. The Sahara, once green, and the Canadian prairies, now becoming a dust bowl, are examples of what happens when soil has no humus.

Skeptics may say that it is not possible to feed the world's burgeoning human population using organic methods. However, farmers in the Orient can produce 4 to 10 times more food per acre than our modern agriculturists. Such a system expends one unit of human energy to produce 50 units of food energy. In contrast, the modern Western agricultural system expends 50 units of fossil energy to produce one unit of food energy. One reason is that excessive energy is consumed in manufacturing nitrogen fertilizer, which is applied heavily in Western commercial agriculture. In nature, the basic nitrogen needs are taken care of adequately by the activity of the soil organisms and different types of plants. Atmospheric nitrogen is fixed or combined in the plants by legumes such as peas, clover and beans as well as by certain nitrogen-fixing bacteria present in healthy, living soil.

There are still other ancient systems of agriculture that can yield far more food per acre than our modern system. One of these is the tier system, in which very high trees shelter the standard-size trees; under these are the bush plants, and then there are lower plants growing on the surface of the soil. Such a procedure, of course, requires ample rainfall and a tropical climate. But it is the ultimate in polycultural methods.

In modern agriculture, much space is wasted between rows of plants to accommodate the heavy machines used, and more space still is wasted at the ends of rows for tractor turning. All that soil is left denuded, exposed to the sun, rain, wind and other destructive forces of erosion, instead of being protected and producing plants to enrich the soil. There is also the tremendous waste of ideal plant food that is being prepared by the activities of soil microorganisms that will not be taken up and incorporated by growing plants but will be washed away by the rain. Furthermore, since there are no plants growing in these spaces, the energy that is being beamed on the soil from the sun and that should be absorbed by the green leaves to purify the atmosphere and eventually to enrich the soil is being lost. In such areas the soil will gradually become more and more impoverished.

Only in recent years has anxiety been expressed over the haphazard and indiscriminate use of inadequately tested chemicals on food crops. The full implication of the cumulative effect of the now-denounced DDT and other chemicals on the living and the unborn, through both ingestion and soil saturation, has never been faced by the public because it has never been revealed by the scientists. But much more is known about the long-term effects of DDT today than when it was first marketed. Surely an overhaul of earth housekeeping is desperately needed.

Over the years, the public has become increasingly aware of the lethal effects of the chemicals that farmers apply to their crops. This greater awareness is due to the efforts of organic growers who have withstood scorn and derision to demonstrate that there is an alternative.

If I write with passion and a sense of urgency, it is because for over fifty years I have worked at improving that most sensitive industry of all—the growing and selling of food fit for human consumption. My standards are high, and they differ in several respects from the supermarket and glossy advertising standards of food value. What I propose is a return to nature's first and basic principles. We may still have time to reverse the degenerative processes already in motion. By revitalizing the soil with organic materials, we can guarantee a never-ending supply of foodstuffs that are fully nutritious, beneficial to the soil and harmless to present and future generations.

Since the publication of the first edition of this book, a whole new generation has been born, and many have a great urge to grow and eat their own organic food. Of course, in the city, people have less space for gardens, and many have no space at all. The role that enthusiastic, organic-minded people must play is to insist on being able to buy organically grown food from the market. It might be in short supply, but more requests will eventually stimulate those who can grow it to increase their efforts to grow more. For people with gardens, a solution is offered in this book. Today the restoration of the soil of our gardens to its natural, unpolluted, vibrant condition is a challenge for all of us.

The organic method is appealing because it is so simple and easy. Any gardener with a little knowledge and an appreciation of the interdependency of soil, plants and animals can grow some food organically. The prime requisite is organic material, which is inexhaustible and in many cases requires only transportation. There is no need to be concerned about trace elements, chemical formulations, pH factor or poison sprays. Just remember that nature alone and unassisted grew the magnificent forests and prairie grasses, with no help from modern chemistry.

You must appreciate and understand the natural cycles of life, however, so that you can use them at the most opportune time and to the fullest extent. Nature may not give us the biggest peach, but it will most certainly give us the most nourishing one whenever soil organisms are thriving. Organic growing is nature's system—the perfect system. Surely we do not expect to be able to improve on nature.

As you follow your growing procedures, keep in mind these seven basic principles of organic growing:
1. Nourish the precious soil with its natural food—organic material.
2. Protect the soil by covering it with organic material at all times.
3. Keep the soil well drained.
4. Permit no trace of unnatural materials to touch the soil.
5. Remember that the birthright of all forms of life in their natural environment is abundant health.
6. Place your footsteps carefully in your garden. If you ever watch

Chinese growers walk through a garden, you will notice that they do not walk abreast, but rather one behind the other, conscious of the fact that footsteps can injure soil.

7. Put your hand lovingly in the soil—let it run through your fingers. Enjoy the feel of it—the woodsy fragrance. Remember it is where you came from. As you hold it in your hands, realize that what you are holding is the foundation of future generations.

Chapter Three
Food and Health

The soil must be kept in good health if the
animal is to remain in good health. The same
is true of man. Soil science is the foundation of
protective medicine, the medicine of tomorrow.

André Voisin

Food—whether chemically or organically grown—should be
judged by the amount of nourishment it provides. Surely this is the
only valid yardstick, simply because nourishment is the very purpose
of food. Yet the measuring of nutritive value not only is an inexact
science but also is of very little interest to the growers and sellers of
our food.

How do wild animals—who are totally dependent on nature—
consume their food? Most species, except carrion-eaters, consume their
food fresh—so fresh, in fact, that it is often still alive. Predators eat
their prey immediately after the kill, and most of them devour it
completely. Should the prey be too large for one meal, it will be either
hidden for future consumption or left for smaller and weaker carnivores
to clean up. Grass-eating animals prefer to graze on the grass as it is
growing rather than the dried hay they are so often given.

But humans seem to be different. Instead of eating fresh food, we
often eat processed food because it is cheaper, more convenient and
easier to handle and store. The purpose of processing is to prevent food

from spoiling by destroying the organisms of decay, but destroying these organisms also destroys the life of the food itself, so it is dead food that we are offered in the beautiful "living-color" packages that cover acres of supermarket shelves.

The increasing quantity of processed food has changed the eating habits of entire nations, and this change has moved us farther and farther away from acquiring true nourishment and from natural, fresh, living food. We show little concern for the quality of long-stored food unless it begins to deteriorate.

Processed or dead food is seen by many consumers as a boon for several reasons. First, such terms as "enriched," "fortified" and "supplemented" on the package imply a nutritional value that guarantees a high standard of health and fitness. That such terms are mainly advertising gimmicks and may refer to the addition of questionable chemicals is glossed over. Second, busy schedules mean that people shop infrequently and appreciate the unlimited shelf life of processed food. What a contrast to the French, Chinese or Italians, who may make separate shopping trips for each meal. It is no coincidence that people from these countries are known for their reverence for food's flavor, freshness and presentation. Third, we have succumbed to the scale of values that puts the dollar at the top. Often the food dollar is the only item in our budgets that is elastic, so it is here that we think we can economize.

Can we possibly have a vigorous, healthy nation nourished by increasing amounts of dead food? With food that is deficient because some of its integral parts have been removed? With food whose very lack of flavor indicates the deficiency of those ingredients necessary for the development of natural flavor? With food that is treated with chemical adulterants and is no longer pure? An investigation of this "battered food" is long overdue. An investigation might resolve the question of why our food needs to be bombarded with more and more chemicals. It might tell us what the long-term effects of these additions and deletions are. We have not yet documented symptoms or diagnosed chemical damage to human cells and tissue caused by the flood of food additives, although recent tests on animals have shown some of them to be carcinogenic.

Scientists tell us that it is possible to destroy an entire species of birds without directly killing even one. Some pesticides interfere with the mechanism for controlling the amount of calcium in an eggshell. When there is not enough calcium, the shell is weak and can easily break during incubation. Other chemicals can inhibit the production of fertile eggs. Rachel Carson in *The Silent Spring* raises concern for bird and animal life because of the effect of such chemicals. Are we not concerned with the damage to human life that could be caused by loading our food with superficially tested chemicals? Do we not have an obligation to future generations to hand the planet's resources down to them in a healthy, viable state? If so, then we must *know* the long-term effects of food adulteration.

Commercial growers and processors are not alone in impoverishing food. The cook blithely pares away vegetable skins so thickly that the valuable layer of concentrated protection against invading microbes is thrown out as waste. Can we afford to discard this protective layer, which might strengthen our own protective layer of skin and immune system, and call it garbage?

Storing or home processing organically grown crops is an effective method of avoiding many of the processed, dead foods our stores offer us. We can continue to enjoy food whose every component is natural even throughout the winter months, when fresh food is costly. Whether garden produce is frozen or canned or served fresh, a minimum of preparation, handling and cooking is desirable.

Food that has not been processed and is subject to natural decay is seldom poisonous—in fact, organisms that cause decay are often used to enhance the texture or flavor of a food. For example, various types of cheese are obtained by natural decaying methods. But the organisms that decay processed or dead food are different, and some can be fatal to humans.

Beauty attracts the eye, but the test of flavor is taste and smell. When offered a choice of foods in the store, we too often base our decision on appearance alone. Contrast this with the grazing habits of animals. The constant movement of grazing animals is evidence of their unceasing search for the most desirable food plants within the limits of their grazing range. Grazing animals choose plants based on flavor and aroma rather than on appearance. Many of us have had the experience of offering what appears to be an especially lush handful of grass to a grazing animal only to have it rejected with a sniff of disapproval as the animal moves on to what looks like a scrubby patch of forage and devours it completely. The proffered grass may have been growing around recent animal droppings, and the high concentration of nitrogen in the droppings may have accelerated the growth of the grass. The animal knows that the grass is not good for it and moves to something that is.

We once conducted an experiment with our Mylora cattle. Given a choice between a pile of supermarket carrots and a pile of Mylora's organically grown carrots, the cattle unanimously clustered at the pile of Mylora carrots, even when we complicated the task by placing a box over the organically grown vegetables. A normal, healthy animal will always choose a balanced, healthful ration.

Two vegetables may appear identical, yet one may boast a protein containing natural substances and be far richer in minerals than the other. A process known as chromophotography will show that there is a difference in crystalline forms between organically and nonorganically grown foods. Such analysis shows the intrinsic difference in a way that regular chemical analysis does not.

Since we cannot chemically analyze our food at every meal, we should eat food we know we can count on. Take our daily orange juice, for example. The recommended daily intake of vitamin C is about 60 milligrams per day. A tumbler of orange juice squeezed at home supposedly contains approximately 60 milligrams. However, if you squeeze your juice from regular commercially grown oranges, you cannot count on that. The oranges may look the same, but they will vary widely in nutritional content, depending on where and when they were picked and on the variety. You may have your glass of juice, but you may not necessarily acquire your needed vitamin C. However, if your juice is squeezed from organically grown oranges, you can at least count on nutritional consistency.

Shoppers buying the largest, most expensive fruits available will often be disappointed by the lack of distinctive flavor in what their eyes tell them should be a premium peach, pear, apple or strawberry. The very lack of taste should indicate something. The least it can tell us is that the produce lacks the substances that produce flavor. Science has no name for these substances, since they have not yet been isolated and analyzed; they could be vitamins, minerals or biological products, such as the amino acids of proteins. Whether these substances are named or not, the fact remains that there is a deficiency, and the consumer cannot obtain the substances that ought to have been there.

Chapter Four
The Soil: Cradle of Life

Precious soil, I say to myself, by what singular custom of law is it that thou wast made to constitute the riches of the freeholder? What should we American farmers be without the distinct possession of that soil? It feeds, it clothes us; from it we draw a great exuberancy, our best meat, our richest drink; the very honey of our bees comes from this privileged spot.

J. Hector St. John (pseudonym for
Michel-Guillaume-Jean de Crèvecoeur)

Previous chapters have outlined the compelling need for change in food production techniques and attitudes, not as a prophecy of doom and gloom, but with the hope of converting growers to the principles of organic cultivation. To reap the rewards of independence and well-being from the soil as de Crèvecoeur did, twentieth-century farmers must arm themselves with a basic knowledge of the land and the teeming life that inhabits and enriches the soil.

Unlike de Crèvecoeur, who farmed an almost-virgin soil, growers today work with soil that has been abused. They must first concentrate on restoring it. By examining its composition and studying nature's ways as described in this chapter, organic growers can adapt their methods to the particular composition of their own land and efficiently overcome whatever problems of pollution or past overcropping it may present.

Geologists tell us that the continuous rains that fell millions of years ago as the earth was cooling produced frequent and heavy flooding. The moving water ground rocks together, producing smaller pieces, which in turn ground together to produce finer and still finer particles. The movement of the great glaciers and extremes of heat and cold played their part in breaking down rocks until the particles reached the size we now recognize as soil. Soil is still being formed by these same processes. As the particles were reduced in size, they were more easily carried along by the water and deposited in depressions on the surface of the earth. These first small plots of soil contained within them minerals essential to life. Louis Bromfield, in *Pleasant Valley,* calls these minerals "the volcanic treasure chest of the subsoil." He brought them to the surface of the soil he cultivated by planting deep-rooted legumes, which tap the source of this mineral wealth. Organic growers who can draw upon this source of nourishment for their crops have a never-ending source of enrichment that is unequaled by any artificial or chemical means.

Life can be divided into three general categories based on where each type lives in relation to the soil. The first category is that of soil organisms, such as insects, bacteria and fungi, many of which are microscopic and live out their lives in the soil without emerging. The second category is vegetable life, which lives partly in the soil and partly out of it. The third category is animal life, which lives almost entirely above the soil.

In nature, despite disparities of size and life expectancy, each of the three forms of life follows essentially the same cycle. Each is born, hatched or sprouted, matures and reproduces, and dies. The forms of life that fall into the first two categories usually die in the same place they lived. As the various forms of life die and come into contact with the earth, the organisms on and in the soil act on the dead material and begin the process of decay. Over countless generations, these dead and decaying organisms add more nutrients to the already-present minerals so that each succeeding generation has had not only more materials in the soil for nourishment but also a greater variety of these materials.

As the composition of the soil became more complex, so did the life forms that depended on it. Plants developed special roots that enabled them to forage farther and farther. These foraging roots search for the tiny crevices in rocks below the soil's surface. When they enter these rocks, the roots are able to glean the minerals stored there, changing the inorganic minerals in rock particles into organic molecules. The plant roots excrete waste substances that act on the rock, bringing such minerals into the chain of life by making them soluble and thus available to the plants.

After the plants die, the soil benefits from the previous physical action of the widespread root system as well as from the decay of organic tissue. The minerals dredged from the subsoil become available to more shallow-rooted plants in the topsoil, and decaying plants add humus content to the soil. Even the dead roots of the plants far beneath the soil furnish food for younger foraging roots as they seek their own special mineral requirements.

In nature, a wide variety of plants and organisms thrives side by side, in an arrangement known as polyculture. Nowhere in nature is there a monocultural pattern, in which only one species of plant is grown to the absolute exclusion of all others. A monocultural pattern occurs only in conventionally cultivated crops. In nature, a mixture of plants growing in the same area can include both tall and low-growing plants. There will be plants that leaf out early in the spring, plants that retain their foliage late into the fall and evergreens that maintain their foliage all winter. These conditions provide dwelling places and protection for many different kinds of insect and animal life. They also provide storage and protection for seeds.

In polyculture, a variety of plants adjacent to one another can harbor insects that maintain a balance between themselves and their surroundings, including those insects we call pests. Provided that there is no thoughtless interference, the insect populations will remain balanced and relatively stable. That is, the predators living in the shelter of soil-covering growth will naturally control the pests that threaten the plants.

In contrast to nature, chemical farmers prepare large fields for planting, and these fields remain bare during the entire cultivation process, sometimes for months, and for about two to three weeks after planting until the seedlings emerge. During this period, many forms of life, both visible and invisible, have no shelter. If poor growing conditions caused by bad weather or inadequate soil preparation check the growth of the new plants, they become more vulnerable to attack by insect pests. The scanty growth will provide poor shelter for the predators of the pest organisms, and these predators will not thrive or be present in sufficient numbers to check the pests. Instead they may be found busily controlling the pests in a neighboring field that offers more hospitable shelter at a crucial stage of their development. Before other possible predators can multiply enough to check the pests in the sparsely grown field, the crop plants may have suffered irreversible damage.

Bare soil poses another threat to the natural balance: erosion. Many of us have heard of the dust bowls of the 1930s in North America. Throughout the centuries, people have left multiple trails of erosion to mark their passing. It is hard to believe that North Africa once boasted lush green fields, which were sacrificed to the voracious needs of the armies of the Roman Empire. The overcropping of this vast area damaged the soil beyond repair by not renewing the humus. The ensuing erosion can be seen today in the shifting sands of the Sahara. Drifting sand spells the death of the soil as well as the people who live on it. Without humus, one wind buries tiny, emerging seedlings and the next exposes their delicate roots to the blazing sun. To reclaim the Sahara and restore the soil to a viable food-producing medium would take several lifetimes and a measure of international dedication beyond any thus far documented in human history. The struggles of Israel to bring the comparatively tiny Negev desert back into production after centuries of erosion give us a yardstick of the effort and devotion required to make "the desert bloom like the rose." Necessity alone can inspire such efforts.

In China, the site of the earth's oldest known civilization, the soil shows great contrasts. Although some areas are shockingly eroded and practically valueless, others, which have been farmed continuously for over four thousand years, are said to be as fertile as ever. Historians credit the philosophy of Buddha, based as it is on a reverence for all forms of life from the lowest to the highest, for the diligent attention and deep respect many generations of Chinese have given to the soil.

The size of particles in soil varies considerably, from coarse gravel to fine clay. Clay particles may even be as fine as face powder. The actual size depends not only on the composition of the parent rock from which the particles came but also on the force and frequency of natural grinding and weathering factors.

It has been estimated that if the outside surfaces of each single particle in an ounce (28 grams) of extremely fine soil were somehow peeled off and laid out on a flat surface, these particles would cover an area of about 6 acres (2.5 hectares). This will give some idea of the feeding area for the plants.

Mineral nutrients become available to plants through the outside surfaces of the soil particles and by way of activities within the soil. Fine soil offers more outside surfaces and has more interspaces for foraging roots than does coarse soil. Furthermore, these interspaces function as extra capillary tubes through which free moisture from the subsoil naturally travels up to the roots of the growing plants.

When rain falls, water gradually fills the spaces between the particles of soil, forcing out the air. As gravity pulls the water down to lower levels, air returns to fill up the spaces again, thus circulating air through the soil. Not all the water is removed by gravity, however. A fine film of water surrounds each particle and is held there by a force called surface tension. This is the important portion of rainwater, for it is this water the plants can use. Just as fine soil holds more nutrients than coarse soil, so does fine soil have a greater water-holding capacity. (This water-holding capacity, incidentally, is increased by adding organic material that holds many times its own weight in water.)

The free water in the soil drains away and eventually enters rivers and finally the ocean. However, when the free water is unable to drain from the topsoil, the passage of air to the roots is blocked and the plant dies of suffocation. It is essential, therefore, that free water be able to drain away quickly so that the plant can breathe. If you dig a hole, remove the soil and then replace all the soil that was removed and broken up, you will not have enough to fill the hole. That empty space at the top of the hole indicates just how much air was present in the healthy soil. Good drainage allows the plants to breathe.

Drainage is important for another reason. Some organisms do not like the warm surface layer. They prefer the deeper soil and cooler areas below the surface. Therefore, the water table must be below the root zone so that inhabitants of all soil levels will thrive. This myriad of organisms is our unpaid workforce, producing food for the roots of plants and creating conditions in the soil that aid root growth. Soil organisms spend a lifetime aerating the soil and manufacturing perfect food for plants.

Minerals present in the rock from which soil is formed are not available to plants, since they are not water soluble, nor do they wash away with the free rainwater. Nature has, however, provided a number of ways to release these minerals to the plant world. One way depends on the air expelled by the microorganisms dwelling in the soil. The carbon dioxide contained in this air dissolves in the moisture surrounding the soil particles and produces carbonic acid. This very weak acid is capable of reacting with minerals that are then used by the foraging roots and sent up through the plant for metabolism. The excreta of soil inhabitants and the waste substances of the roots themselves also help change minerals into solutions that plants can use.

These natural activities are greatly accelerated during the growing season. Roots, developing rapidly in the warm, moist soil, greedily seize on the available plant food before it can be washed away by the rains. The roots then develop burgeoning systems to forage farther afield for the trace minerals that are so important for their optimum development.

Mulching is the practice of placing materials on the surface of the soil, leaving the top layer of soil undisturbed. Mulch keeps the soil moist and increases air supply to the organisms living in the top layer of soil. This greater supply of air motivates the organisms to produce more of nature's own special food for hungry plant roots. Under a hay or straw mulch, new roots of plants grow profusely between the soil and the mulch, as well as in the soil itself. The soil under the mulch provides ideal conditions for the development of plant roots, and they thrive on the extra food thus made available. You will see ample evidence of this if you carefully lift the mulch up and observe the plant roots and the various soil inhabitants that have taken up residence there.

As well as providing a nurturing environment for the organisms in the soil, mulching helps regulate the movement of moisture. The water that clings tightly to the soil particles is removed in two ways: (1) It is absorbed by the roots of plants and then passes up the stems into the growing leaves, carrying with it the soil nutrients, which become incorporated into the plant. Then the moisture evaporates from the leaves. (2) It evaporates directly from the surface of the soil where it contacts warm, drier air. The rapid evaporation of water directly from the soil in this way can be checked by impeding the free movement of dry, atmospheric air through the soil. This can be done by breaking the topsoil down to a powdery consistency with a hoe or rake and spreading it so as to provide a complete cover for the surface of the soil. A dust mulch effectively prevents evaporation, but it has the disadvantage of becoming too dry and inhospitable for the plant roots to function properly. Other forms of soil cover, such as straw, hay or compost, are just as effective without this drawback. In fact, they offer numerous advantages beyond the actual retention of moisture.

When soil forms, layers of dead and decaying vegetable and animal matter constitute an excellent mat to check evaporation. They also eventually add an extra source of nourishment. Musty hay, dead leaves, grass clippings or even the lowest grade of fir or hemlock sawdust—

all organic materials—can produce a similar effect. Among these, sawdust alone presents a problem. The organisms that decay sawdust require additional soil nitrogen and so impoverish plants unless they are supplemented. Sawdust can be so fine in texture that it is easily mixed with the topsoil. If this mixing occurs before the sawdust has completely decomposed, the crops planted in it will suffer from a lack of nitrogen and become yellow and unhealthy. Hay and straw, however, do not present the same problem, since they decompose more quickly and are not as easily mixed with soil. Some commercial growers use a thin plastic sheeting for ground cover, but it adds nothing to the soil and is difficult to dispose of.

Poor farming methods can damage the soil and create conditions in which large populations of undesirable organisms and insect pests overwhelm valuable crops. Instead of thoroughly evaluating the soil and changing their agricultural methods, some worried farmers turn to soil fumigation as a quick method of re-establishing their control over the situation. In farm fields, soil fumigation is usually accomplished by pulling an implement with cultivator tines through loosened topsoil. A chemical is forced down through tubes in the cultivator tines to escape into the loosened soil. The fumes of the chemical then dissipate upwards throughout the soil mass and destroy the pest. Fumigants affect the various forms of life in the soil in many different ways. Some organisms are killed, some are damaged or develop mutations, and others are not affected at all.

Two major problems follow soil fumigation. First, some predators that naturally control the pest may be more sensitive than the pest to the fumigating agent. If so, any future natural control of the pest by that predator will be thwarted. Second, any pest arriving in the area after the fumigation may not be accompanied by its natural enemy/predator. For the immediate future, it may reign supreme and uncontrolled.

Fumigation is at best a short-lived expedient. Before too long, farmers are faced with choosing other fumigating procedures or changing over to entirely different kinds of crops not threatened by the pests they cannot control. This decision can be costly. In addition, there may be no other crop suitable to the particular locale that could bring an adequate financial return. Under our present profit-oriented system of food production, there seems to be little choice for farmers whose soil has been damaged by poor farming methods. The one thing that would benefit everyone in the long run, growing soil-improving crops to restore the natural balance to their fields, costs too much. This makes soil fumigation, the short-term "remedy," appear to be a desirable solution, when in the long term it can prove disastrous.

Another short-sighted solution is the use of chemical plant food. Commercial growers place chemicals in the root zone to stimulate plant growth and thus increase crop yield. This practice is detrimental to both soil and the plants growing in it: some of the organisms become less active, whereas other organisms are stimulated to greater activity, consuming more organic material and eventually using it up without replenishing the supply. The stimulation provided by chemical plant food is temporary, artificial and does not satisfy the natural food requirements of the soil organisms or the plants. In order to seek food, plant roots naturally thrust through the soil. Coming upon a chemical bonanza in their root zone, however, the plants halt this search for vital trace minerals found in the soil beyond. Having stopped to feast on the artificial plant food, the plants are now nutritionally deficient despite an appearance of vigor. Scientists have found that the soil becomes deficient as well.

Have you ever noticed that when you leave something on the soil surface, such as a box or a sack, and then remove it a few days later, many different forms of life will have discovered this protected haven and moved into it? The most fertile part of the soil is the area immediately below the dust mulch on the surface. If the surface is protected by a mulch of leaves or other vegetable matter, then the richest soil is immediately below this protected area. For this reason, soil cultivation should be minimal.

Nature maintains a moist and loose soil surface by means of a natural mulch of vegetable and animal remains. The crumblike structure of soil, when undisturbed, allows free movement of air in the noncompacted soil mass. The mulch lying on the surface prevents the air in the soil from coming in contact with drier, moving, atmospheric air that would, by increasing evaporation, dry the soil.

Millions of soil microbes under the surface of a mulch are protected from the sun, the wind, the rain and predators. When they die, their remains enrich the soil. New seedlings germinate under protective surface vegetation and soon discover this new source of food. In this way, plants benefit from generations of microbes.

Modern agriculture treats these organisms badly. Although a freshly plowed or clean, cultivated field looks neat and tidy, during the winter, it is extremely vulnerable. Just watch that bare field as the wet season progresses—the rains wash the fine soil particles to the lower areas, where they form silt, which plugs up the little holes and cracks that have developed during the summer. These plugged holes and cracks effectively make small dams, so water cannot drain into the subsoil. As the winter progresses, the field gradually accumulates a series of small dams, which get bigger and bigger until many of them merge into lakes. No plants can grow there. The silt excludes air from the soil, suffocating plants and preventing them from absorbing energy from the sun. There is no growth to absorb the plant food that is released by soil organisms. That food washes away and is lost.

It is not always easy to relate cause and effect in agriculture, because the cause is usually far removed from the effect, both in time and in place. I can illustrate this with two examples from our experience at Mylora.

The first one involved an area of about 2 acres (0.8 hectare), which boasted about 20 fruit trees, mostly apple, but also Damson plum trees, Bartlett pears and Bing cherries. Our small herd of cattle grazed in this area and on warm summer days, peacefully chewed their cud in the shade of the trees.

This idyllic scene was marred by caterpillars. Caterpillar moths lay eggs on tree branches in the autumn. The next spring, the caterpillars hatch and feed voraciously on the leaves of the trees. This was happening in our fruit trees, and we had to keep a close watch and destroy any nests as soon as we saw them start to hatch. Occasionally we missed some, and the caterpillars ate many leaves before we noticed them.

Observing that the grass under the trees was eaten bare and the ground trampled and packed by the hoofs of our cattle, I suddenly realized that trees growing in their natural habitat would have a soft decaying layer of leaves on the ground as far out as the branches extended. Under that soft layer of leaves would be a supply of almost-decayed leaves next to the soil. How different from the bare, hard ground under our apple trees. The ground was so dry that their roots could not get any nourishment from it and had to forage deeper in the moist lower but poorer soil. Perhaps if we improved the soil, the trees would become healthier and the caterpillars would be eliminated.

The easiest solution was to simulate natural conditions. We used truckloads of hemlock and fir sawdust to build up a layer 6 to 8 inches (15 to 20 centimetres) thick to cover and protect the soil. This layer was spread on top of the soil as far as the tree's branches extended. Digging into the sawdust after a month or more, we could easily see the larger soil organisms that had arrived, as well as tiny new roots from the tree, all seeking this coveted area. As the soil became richer, warmer and teeming with life, the apple trees became healthier and were no longer so appealing to the caterpillars. After two or three years, we had no more caterpillars on the fruit trees, and our cattle still enjoyed the shade and continued to chew their cud on the soft sawdust.

The second example involved a field where one year we grew a crop of carrots, the next year a crop of peas and the following year a crop of oats. To inspect the oat crop as it was being harvested, I had to climb on top of the combine because the oat straw was over 5 feet (1.5 metres) high. From that vantage point, it was strikingly noticeable that there were parallel rows running the length of the field in which the plants were not as tall as the rest. The depressed rows corresponded to the tractor's wheel marks between the rows where the carrots had grown two years earlier. That year had been wet, and we had had to cultivate the carrots more often than usual. All those extra trips on the vulnerable damp soil with the tractor had caused enough damage to the soil structure to be obvious two years later. The depressed growth resulted from the compacted soil. Because of the nature of the pea crop, which grows unevenly, the depressed growth areas had not been visible earlier, and we were unaware of the dramatic damage until the oat crop showed the evidence. It is impossible by mechanical means to restore the soil structure, especially when it has been compacted while still damp. Machines can only break up hard lumps. The structure can only be restored by the action of living organisms in the soil, and these are organisms that most growers ignore or even destroy.

The inhabitants of a really fertile soil are so numerous that one handful of soil can contain more organisms than there are people on the face of the earth. The weight of the organisms in one field of highly fertile soil can be greater than the weight of all the domestic animals that can be fed from food grown on that field. The variety of these organisms is astounding. They include worms, fungi, insects and bacteria, all of which depend for nourishment on the decaying remains of previous generations of plants and animals. In turn, they convert the refuse in which they live into ideal plant food that is easily accessible to the roots of the growing plants.

The substances exuded by various organisms in the soil react with the mineral content of the fine rock particles to make plant food available. They also serve the soil in another capacity. Some of these exuded substances are like glue and enable masses of fine particles of soil to adhere to one another in highly irregular forms. Because their irregular shape and apparently haphazard construction allow them to touch at relatively few points, these conglomerations of fine particles don't compact. In this way, the soil maintains its efficient structure, which resembles a slice of well-leavened bread rather than a slice of chilled butter.

In cultivating the soil by natural processes, various organisms perform special functions. The most active cultivators are earthworms. They travel endlessly through the soil, making tunnels the diameter of their bodies as they go. In order to travel, they eat their way through the soil. Their digestive juices react with the soil particles they eat, and their muscular contractions move the particles along the digestive tube, grinding one particle against the other and exposing more of the oxidized mineral surfaces to the action of the digestive juices. When the earthworms travel from the subsoil to the surface soil, they bring some of the subsoil with them. Having been through the digestive tract, this subsoil is already prepared for incorporation into the topsoil when it is deposited on the surface.

If you look carefully at your soil, you may observe the little piles of worm casts. They are five times richer in nitrogen, seven times richer in phosphoric acid and eleven times richer in potash than the surrounding soil, which has not been through the intestines of earthworms. You will notice that these casts maintain their shape through many weeks of rain, whereas other, ordinary little piles of soil are washed flat after a few heavy rains. A moderate earthworm population will annually bring about 10 tons of castings, rich in prepared minerals, to the surface of each acre of fertile soil (about 26 tons per hectare). It has been calculated that in the rich valley of the White Nile, earthworms bring to the surface 120 tons of castings per acre (305 tons per hectare) during the six-month growing season.

What are the indications of a satisfactory earthworm population? Evidence of one earthworm per shovelful is considered enough to ensure the continuation of this valuable form of cultivation and soil enrichment.

Earthworm tunnels throughout the soil provide free access for air, water and plant roots. The earthworm lines the tunnels with sticky excretions from its body, which help to hold the tunnel walls intact and to reinforce them against collapsing.

The excretions of earthworms seem to be attractive to the plant roots, since the roots travel along the tunnels, growing vigorously as they do so. Fungi also grow abundantly in these soil tunnels, and larger insects burrow between the roots and loosen the soil without damaging the roots, adding further to this natural type of cultivation. Such forms of cultivation cannot be duplicated by humans or machines. We merely stir the surface of the soil in a way that tends to dry it and make it less suitable for nourishing plant roots. People have interfered with natural cycles since they began to cultivate the soil. Organic material was displaced because people deposited their food wastes away from where food was grown. As people multiplied, soil depletion increased. This increasing loss of organic material constitutes a real threat to our future.

As great quantities of food move from vast farms to densely populated areas, reckless handling of food wastes is augmenting urban pollution while soil in the producing area starves for the nutriment of the vegetative wastes that are flushed away in garburetors or sent to landfills.

Human excrement has been efficiently used to grow food by various societies for centuries. Modern society, however, considers such a procedure esthetically offensive, while at the same time it rationalizes—because of cost—the dumping of virtually raw sewage into rivers and other waters upstream from inhabitants who must use this water for drinking. Surely common sense and the concept spelled out in Sir Albert Howard's Law of Return (that everything that comes from the soil must be returned to the soil) dictate that the disposal area for sewage belongs in the fields that grow the crops. The cost of returning such wastes to the farm field today must be calculated against the far higher costs of renewing the quality of our soil, air and water tomorrow. A few cities do process their sewage and sell it to growers, but most cities unthinkingly dispose of it as cheaply as possible, with absolute lack of concern for posterity.

In the past, sewage disposal was relatively simple, but now the presence of heavy metals and a chemical residue of toxic materials make the solution more difficult and more expensive. If this situation is further delayed while society continues to industrialize and add to its problems, it may well become impossible to handle.

The safest way to prevent the spread of disease that could result from the use of human excrement is to destroy the pathogens by careful composting. The proportions must be correct, and excrement must undergo the high temperatures generated after the pile is first assembled and then again when it is repiled. Alternatively, human waste can be safely used in its raw state on nonfood crops. People of earlier cultures were successful in doing this. Why can't we be?

Many forms of life exist in fertile soil. Some can move as freely as they wish, whereas others are immobile and must be carried by agents such as water or insects. In this immobile group are those that thrive close to the soil surface, where there is a greater amount of light, warmer temperatures and the continued presence of air. Others require opposite conditions, that is, less air, cooler temperatures and intense darkness. Each inhabits the particular area of the soil that provides the optimum condition for its well-being.

A moldboard plow turns the soil upside down as it cuts through the soil. In doing so, it damages whole cultures of microorganic life. Those that are accustomed to dwelling in the cellar find themselves in the penthouse, and vice versa. Organisms thus removed from their normal living conditions show sharply reduced activity and consequently provide less food to maintain the well-being of the plants. Plowing is responsible for destroying vast networks of tunnels through the soil, thus grossly interfering with root growth and preventing the prompt drainage that is essential after heavy rains.

There seem to be some advantages to plowing. The advantage of the moldboard plow is its effectiveness in burying the surface trash— undecomposed vegetation. The resulting clean surface soil permits seeding implements to operate freely. As the plow turns the soil over, it loosens the particles, moving them against one another. Its actions might be compared to that of bending a book so that the pages are moved one against the other. In this respect, it is physically very effective.

The mechanical advantage of the moldboard plow is far outweighed by its biological disadvantage. Many years ago, at Mylora, we stopped using the plow to invert the soil. Instead we used a rototiller to chop up the surface vegetation and an implement called a subsoiler to break up the soil below the rototilled layer. If there was not too much surface trash, we used a cultivator or disc harrows to make the surface soil fine enough for seeding.

If your soil is poor because it is too coarse and sandy and will not hold moisture, the addition of fine clay soil will help. Conversely, if the soil is too heavy and stiff, it will be easier to work with if you add some coarse sand. You must make sure, however, that these soil additives are not of questionable origin, that is, that they have not been subjected to any form of pollution. Such materials will certainly improve the physical structure of your soil. If, however, they involve considerable financial outlay, then that same money would give better returns invested in barnyard manure and in growing green manure crops to improve that most important factor—the life in the soil. Barnyard manure will also improve the soil's physical texture. Seaweed is another minerally rich additive that does an excellent job of improving soil. Applying well-decomposed organic material to the soil annually is the best way to increase soil fertility.

The force of falling raindrops is absorbed by plant leaves, which temporarily bend under the impact and then return unharmed to their normal position. The raindrops then fall more gently to the next leaf below, while most of the water runs down the stalk of the plant to the soil, trickling through the protective mass of vegetation. It percolates through the minuscule tunnels in the soil engineered by the worms and insects and then seeps to the lower levels of the soil and eventually to the deeper drainage canals.

If the soil is fertile and protected by natural vegetation, the drainage water will be clear. Furthermore, it will not become muddy even as it travels through the soil because the sticky insect excretions that maintain the crumblike structure of the soil are resistant to the water. Rain damages soil that is not protected by organic materials and lacks the drainage tunnels left by burrowing insects and decaying roots. The surface particles are loosened and the soil beneath is compacted. It is the loosened particles of damaged soil that give the water a muddy appearance as they are carried along. When the movement of the water slows down, this vital component of once-fertile soil ends up as silt on the bottom of a river or pond. Standing water on the surface of the soil or sluggish movement of water is always damaging and must be eliminated because the silt plugs the natural drainage holes.

The daily creed of organic growers is to respect the soil that nourishes them and their families, laboring now so that they may hand on to those who follow them a soil of everlasting excellence.

Chapter Five
Plants

Flower in the crannied wall,
I pluck you out of the crannies,
I hold you here, root and all, in my hand,
Little flower—but if I could understand,
What you are, root and all, and all in all,
I should know what God and man is.

Alfred, Lord Tennyson

Plants provide the vital link between the energy generated by the sun and the energy demands of people and animals. Not only is energy necessary for physical well-being, reproductive vigor and resistance to disease, but for humans, whose continuing creative and intellectual progress is dependent on the quality of their food, the goodness of plants is crucial. In addition to providing us with energy when we consume them as food, plants have the highly specialized function of keeping the quality of the air constant by continuously regenerating the oxygen supply.

A plant absorbs moisture from the soil through the outside layer or protective covering of its fine, hairlike roots. The passage of this nutrient-carrying moisture through the semipermeable membranes of the roots is called osmosis. When a plant is healthy and vigorous, its leaves are wide open to the sun, transpiring moisture into the atmosphere. The nutrients that the moisture has carried from the soil are left behind in the plant.

When the plants are eaten, the carbon contained in the plants provides energy and heat to the consumer. Some of this carbon is changed into carbon dioxide, which is exhaled into the atmosphere from the lungs. Plants use the carbon content of this carbon dioxide to grow more green leaves, and at the same time they release the oxygen so that it can be used once again by animals. This continuous cycling of the carbon and oxygen via plants and animals maintains a constant amount of oxygen in the atmosphere.

For a plant to function efficiently, all of its environmental requirements and nutritional needs must be met. Only then can it develop fully and provide suitable nourishment for animals. We can control some of these requirements, such as the nutrients available for plants, but we have only limited control over others. For instance, we can choose to grow plants on the north or south side of a building. We may have a choice of a heavy or light soil. We can choose plants that take a long time or a short time to mature. We can sow seeds early in the spring or late in the spring. We cannot change the climate, however.

Excessive moisture can be drained from low areas of land, and too little moisture can be rectified by irrigation. Diagnosing moisture deficiency is fairly simple, since most plants display definite symptoms when they are short of water. The most common and most obvious symptom is the wilting of the leaves, which is a protective device for the plant. When the leaves wilt and turn down away from the sun, they are conserving the moisture that remains in the body of the plant so that the entire plant will not become dehydrated and die.

Here is a simple test to determine the quantity of moisture in clay soil. Take a handful of soil, squeeze it tightly and then release the pressure. If water drips from the soil, the soil is too wet. If you can see little sparkles of moisture as you hold it to the light, the soil has all the moisture it can contain. If you release the pressure, and the handful of soil loses its shape and crumbles, it is too dry.

When there is a deficiency of nutrients reaching a plant, there may be indications that all is not well, but identifying the exact nature of the deficiency may be difficult. General symptoms of nutrient deficiency are small size, slow growth, unnatural leaf color and a proliferation of small leaves. None of these symptoms can be definitely related to a particular deficiency, although the yellowing of the leaves usually indicates a nitrogen deficiency. Magnesium deficiency in corn plants can be recognized by yellowish white stripes in a regular pattern along the length of the leaves. Black spots throughout the fleshy roots of beets indicate boron deficiency; these are more prominent in larger beets, whereas they do not show up so much in smaller beets. Such symptoms could also be caused by other problems, such as physical damage to the root system by faulty cultivation or by diseases or even lack of moisture. There are so many requirements for plants that it is practically impossible to recognize many deficiencies without the aid of soil scientists with their special knowledge and equipment.

A scientific soil analysis can determine some nutrient deficiencies, and usually the scientists will then recommend synthetic plant foods to be applied to the affected crops. However, scientists judge the success of such a procedure by the quantity of the crops produced, not by their nutritional quality. This procedure is further limited by the incomplete knowledge scientists have about the proportion of soil elements that plants require.

Three hundred years ago, Jean Van Helmont, a Belgian chemist and physician, planted a 5-pound (2.3-kilogram) willow tree in 200 pounds (91 kilograms) of dry earth. For five years, he added nothing but rainwater to the soil, and his tree grew until it weighed 169 pounds (77 kilograms). The soil was dried and reweighed and was found to have lost only 2 ounces (57 grams); a mere 2 ounces (57 grams) of soil was consumed in growing 169 pounds (77 kilograms) of tree. The soil therefore was depleted of very little mineral. We have to wonder, then, why such vast quantities of chemical plant foods are used in modern agriculture.

Fortunately, organic growers do not have to concern themselves with such contradictions. They provide adequate nourishment for their unpaid workers—the living organisms in the soil—and their deficiency problems are solved.

Plant roots growing through the soil absorb the nutrients they need for their development, but they also give off their waste products, or exudates, to the soil. The organisms, seeds and plants that are in the soil are affected in various ways by exudates. Too many of the same species of plants growing beside one another can create an undesirable or even intolerable level of pollution as a result of the accumulation of their particular waste products. Conversely, the exudates of one type of plant can be stimulants for plants of another species and provide nourishment for their searching roots. Nature makes good use of this factor, as can be seen by the different kinds of plants that grow with their roots intertwined. This is symbiosis.

Knowing how the exudates of specific plants affect one another is invaluable information to organic growers, who will then be able to plant their crops to the greatest advantage. At present, we do know that marigold roots have a depressing effect on the verticillium wilt fungus, asparagus roots exude a substance that is toxic to nematodes, and witch weed germinates only in the presence of stimulants exuded by corn and a few other plants.

In England at the time of the Industrial Revolution, farmers found that if they grew different crops in succeeding seasons in each of their fields, yields were increased and disease was dramatically reduced. This break with the traditional method of planting the same kind of crop in the same field, year after year and even generation after generation, was an important milestone in the history of agriculture. Yet the reasons for its successes are still a subject for argument. The reason advanced at that time was that the continuous growing of one type of plant in an area used up too much of certain nutrients in the soil and that these nutrients would thus be in shorter supply with each successive growing year. Undoubtedly depletion of nutrients can be a contributing factor, but a more basic cause seems to be pollution of the soil by plant exudates. Even casual gardeners know the frustration of seeing the weeds that have escaped the hoe flourish with far greater vigor than a carefully tended crop. It is probable that the weeds are being stimulated by the exudates of the crop plants, which are themselves being stifled by their own pollutants.

Nature takes care of soil building, sanitation and pest control by means of polyculture. As many plants of different species grow adjacent to one another, they in effect tend one another. In contrast, most farmers, bound by economics, cling to the convenient monocultural system and are forced to treat each problem separately. Organic growers attempt, as far as possible, to copy nature and practice polyculture. Their reward is soil that grows vigorous plants to nourish healthy people.

There is another vital, but almost completely overlooked, way in which plants obtain nourishment from the soil. Known as mycorrhizal association, it involves a special type of root fungus, the mycorrhiza. This fungus grows on decaying matter in the soil, and it nourishes the growing plant with the decaying matter. The fine threads of fungus—the mycelia—are attracted by the roots of the plants and grow toward them. One type of mycorrhiza grows around the root and attaches itself to the outside of the root, whereas another type grows inside and between the cells of the roots. Both the plant root and the fungus benefit by this invasion. The mycorrhiza appears to obtain more nourishment from the surrounding soil when it is growing in association with the plant root, and the plant root actually digests the fungus. Since it is very rich in protein, the mycorrhiza provides a living bridge of protein between the dead and decaying remains of previous generations of plant and animal life and the new and developing plant. The mycorrhizal association is considered by some scientists to be the source of protein that provides the plant with resistance to its natural enemies—insects and disease. It is another example of a symbiotic relationship.

Modern discoveries of wonder drugs have spotlighted lowly fungi and forced people to depend on these diligent workers for medicine. Perhaps it is logical that the contributions of a fungus should be available to people through their daily food if that food is raised the natural way, the organic way, since this fungus will only flourish and fulfill its bridging role in soil that is well supplied with organic matter. Soils that have recently been sterilized or had heavy applications of chemicals will not provide conditions suitable for mycorrhizal development. Without the mycorrhizal association, plants' immune systems suffer. If plant immune systems are weak, can they help develop the immune systems of their consumers?

When plant roots are supplied with nutrients by artificial plant food placed close around them, they do not have to forage through the soil as widely as they normally would. There is then the distinct possibility that the plant will fail to obtain some of the nutrients valuable to it that are present in the soil but not in the artificial plant food. In addition, the price of using chemical fertilizer is a steady loss of nitrogen in the soil. When chemicals are used, the natural bacteria that fix atmospheric nitrogen become less active or die. In one case, in an attempt to counteract this loss of nitrogen, spinach growers used heavy concentrations of nitrate fertilizer and produced plants with greatly increased foliage. The improved yield of the crop undoubtedly resulted in increased sales for the growers; however, excess nitrates in spinach are said to have poisoned children in Germany and France, and our own press has reported similar deaths in Eastern Canada.

Potash and phosphoric acid are two other major chemical plant foods. These substances are mined from natural deposits in the earth that accumulated very slowly over a long period of time and must be regarded as part of our capital heritage. If one continually draws on capital at a greater rate than it is replaced, it eventually becomes depleted.

To nourish a steadily increasing population, we must find some source of plant food that will increase as the population increases; otherwise, we shall find ourselves in the position of trying to make a decreasing supply of plant food fill an ever-increasing need. In the natural cycle of life, waste products from previous generations of all forms of life provide the sustenance for new life. (See Diagram 1, page 29.) Nature's scheme is most logical and practical in these crucial times, especially now, when pollution by waste products is an omnipresent threat.

Plants are usually divided into three basic categories: annuals, biennials and perennials. Annuals are plants that grow from seed and reproduce seed in the same growing season—peas, tomatoes, cucumbers and corn are all annuals. Biennials are plants that store up food in a root or head in the first season and then send up seed stalks to produce seed the following season. They include carrots, beets, onions and cabbage. Perennials do not usually produce seeds until the third year, and thereafter will produce seed every year; examples are rhubarb and asparagus.

Occasionally a plant from one of these groups will take on the characteristics of another group; "bolters" are an example in the biennial category. An individual biennial may produce seed in the first year as though it were an annual, but the food portion, that is, the root, fails to develop and becomes woody and inedible. This plant is a mutant. Such a mutant carrot or beet should be culled, even though the seed stalk towers over the other biennials in the field. Experience has shown that planting such seeds in the following season produces more mutations.

Many people have bought tulip bulbs that grew beautifully the first year and had large, exquisite blooms only to find that bulbs from those blooms did not produce satisfactory blooms in the following years. Most people blame themselves for some error they committed in growing them, not realizing that these beautiful blooms were hybrids, which lack reproductive stability.

Mutations and hybrids are similar. The difference is that mutations occur naturally, whereas hybrids are the result of human intervention to the regenerative system of any form of life.

To develop a hybrid, the scientist must first shelter the pistil or female part of the flower so that neither its own pollen nor that of any other plant can come in contact with it and thus fertilize it. The scientist then introduces pollen from another specially selected plant to fertilize the sheltered pistil, which develops into a seed called a hybrid. This operation is designed to develop certain supposedly desirable characteristics—for example, to make apples a deeper red color, to give tomatoes a tougher skin, or to put more peas in the pod. The results of such experimental unions vary widely. Reproduction is most fruitful, however, and many seeds are formed. Such seeds are planted and developed to maturity, and their new characteristics are carefully noted. Occasionally one is found with a highly desirable characteristic, to the great joy of the scientist.

A mutant or open-pollinated plant results when the pistil is left unprotected and nature performs the fertilization. This newly generated plant is subjected to the rigors of the weather as well as its natural enemies, insects and disease. With such weapons and other natural pitfalls, nature culls most severely to provide the finest nourishment for life. As the open-pollinated plants grow and mature, ripened seeds fall to the ground and germinate. Only a very few actually grow into mature plants. Again, as an enactment of the law of survival of the fittest, nature culls them as they go through their lives so that only the best adapt and survive.

In human-induced fertilization the seed lives a pampered life, as the scientist nurses it along in a greenhouse or nursery, using all types of artificial plant foods for nourishment and chemicals for protection. Such a plant is never exposed to the harshness of nature and does not experience nature's culling. Hybrids themselves can produce many variations and so lack stability. Thus, the new plants have to be continuously bred again to produce good crops. How can scientists guarantee that such food plants, untried by nature, will survive through generations and will provide us with adequate nourishment? The value of the whole breeding process is in question: one small oversight can result in massive crop losses and starvation.

Plant reproduction is accomplished in a number of different ways. The majority of vegetable plants are annuals that reproduce sexually. The male part of the flower, the pollen, must come in contact with the female part, the pistil, which then grows and develops into seed. Some flowers have male and female parts contained in one bloom. These are called complete flowers, and pollination is accomplished when the male part meets the female part. In other plants the male and female parts are segregated in different areas of the same plant. Corn, for example, carries the male flower on the top of erect stems. The developing cob is situated partway up the stem of the corn plant. The pollen must fall onto each of the silken strands that flow out of the cob and then travel along these strands into the kernels inside the cob in order to complete pollination. If any of the silken threads are missed, the kernels to which they are attached will not be pollinated and therefore will not develop. A single row of corn planted across the direction of the prevailing wind would be poorly pollinated because the wind is apt to drift the pollen sideways. By the time the pollen falls down to the level of the corn silks, it will have been blown some distance away from the plant. Thus, knowledgeable growers never plant corn in single rows.

Plants that have male and female parts in separate flowers, such as cucumbers and squash, and plants that carry the male flower on one plant and the female on another usually require the services of the wind or insects for pollination. They need these agents to carry the pollen to the pistil, especially if they are not planted closely. Plants that put forth an abundance of blooms yet develop few, if any, seeds are victims of incomplete pollination. Fruit trees that display lopsided or unevenly developed fruit, nubby or seedy strawberries, and pea pods containing less than their full complement of peas are all further evidence of incomplete pollination.

Plants that reproduce sexually will vary, just as brothers and sisters have quite different characteristics. Changes in plant characteristics can occur gradually and, as we have seen in the case of bolters, mutants may show up in any crop. Seed growers must be always on the alert for variants with undesirable qualities, culling them and destroying their seeds to prevent the propagation of their undesirable characteristics in the following season's crop.

Another type of plant reproduction is the vegetative or asexual method. Dahlias, tulips, daffodils, garlic and horseradish either grow small bulbs around the base of the mother bulb or the mother bulb itself divides into smaller bulbs, each of which is a new, individual plant, which can be set out separately. Strawberry plants send out shoots called runners from the mother plant. These runners develop strong roots, which thrust downwards into the soil. At the same point, they send up leaf shoots and a new, independent plant is born. Mint plants grow heavy, lateral roots just under the surface of the soil and at a short distance from the mother plant. They also send up leaves that form a new plant. Rhubarb has a large pulpy root with a number of growing points called crowns. As the plant develops, the size of the root increases, and it can be divided so that each of the growing points can be set out as a separate plant. Plants reproduced asexually seldom vary from the mother plant, whereas sexually reproduced plants will never be exactly the same as each other or the mature plants from whose seed or seeds they have developed.

Some shrubs and fruit trees are reproduced in still another way. Layering is a procedure in which a branch long enough to reach the ground is anchored into the soil, but the growing tip is left uncovered. In time the anchored area will develop roots, and the growing tip will develop into a normal plant. At the end of the season the new plant can be severed from the main plant and moved to another part of the garden.

Another method is to use cuttings. Cuttings are short pieces of mature wood from the previous season's growth. They can be set directly into the soil after all but one or two buds at the top of the cutting have been removed. The cutting develops roots in the soil, and the buds form the top growth for the new plant.

Very choice fruit trees and rosebushes are accorded still different treatment. These varieties may have been bred for unusual color, size of bloom or multiplicity of fruit and may have acquired their special qualities at the expense of vigor. Some sturdiness can be restored by joining them to an unrefined, vigorous member of the same family with a strong rooting system. For example, the root of a wild briar is commonly used for strengthening delicate rose plants using this method, which is called budding.

Chapter Six
Pests and Pesticides

*Nearly all the abuses he [man] inflicts on the
soil, plants and animals are returned to him in
kind, perhaps indirectly, but all the more
malignantly because the damage is often far
advanced before it can be seen and corrected.*

Lewis Herber

Having explored plant growth cycles and the natural method
of soil rebuilding, we can clearly see how those who follow organic
or natural methods differ in their thinking from those who follow
conventional agricultural methods. Because organic growers follow
nature's ways, they take the long-term view in planning, planting and
protecting their land and resources. Consequently, their attitudes differ
drastically from those of chemical farmers, and their definitions of such
terms as "weed" and "pest" are not blanket denunciations but depend
on the functions that the pests perform. Organic growers also believe
that common errors in managing the soil and growing plants are the
result of techniques powered by the need for short-term economic profit.

At Mylora, we operated on the principle that the main purpose of
growing food plants is to adequately nourish people and, of course,
to earn a livelihood. When we were farming, we knew that the produce
we grew was both free of poisonous materials and as nourishing as
possible.

We always regarded so-called pests as nature's censors and so resisted the blandishments of the chemical companies, because we saw no advantage in the wholesale destruction of pests. We knew that normally our vigorously growing, healthy plants were not harmed by pests. We also knew that the converse was true: that sickly plants would attract destructive pests. The destruction of plants by pests is really an enactment of nature's law of survival of the fittest. It is a ruthless law, but the culling of weaklings allows the quality and strength of the species to improve, for only the specimens best suited to the environment live to reproduce.

However, profit-oriented growers cannot tolerate the losses occasioned by nature's destruction of unfit plants, so they protect such unfit plants from "pests." They believe that nurturing these second-rate plants will be economically feasible, even though it is an unsound agricultural and nutritional practice.

The very word "pest" has an almost completely negative connotation. Yet in the vast world of the multitudinous pests, it is impossible to divide them into "good guys" and "bad guys," as we shall see in an exploration of insects, bacteria, fungi, viruses and weeds, all of which can destroy or help food crops, depending on the circumstances. It is agricultural mismanagement that permits crops to be destroyed by pests, and analysis of massive crop failures usually shows that the pests had everything but an engraved invitation to come in and do their worst.

History shows that agricultural efforts have always been beset by pests to some extent. In ancient times, serious outbreaks of pests were so rare that they were attributed to the wrath of gods brought down because of some human offense. In the biblical recounting of the plague of locusts, and in stories of crop failures in Greek and Roman vineyards, the disasters could usually be attributed to breaches of the moral code. It is only in the past century that we have come to recognize that agricultural disasters are attributable to a breach of the laws of nature. They are of our own making.

"Multiplication of insects and their devastations are largely incited by the degeneracy in our plants and the badness of our culture," wrote Horace Greeley, the American journalist, in 1870. Approximately seventy years later, Sir Albert Howard published his principles of natural plant growing, in which he maintained that the plants themselves should be able to resist their natural enemies, insects and disease. Observant farmers recognize that pest problems can usually be traced to areas where the soil conditions are not ideal. Low spots with poor drainage can become breeding grounds for pests. Fungi can flourish on plants grown where there are excessive amounts of organic materials, because the materials have not been changed by nature into a form of food that the plants can use.

Insects live above and below the soil surface and are visible in such profusion at some seasons that it might seem that they could take over the earth. Relatively few species of insects attack food crops, however. The massive chemical assault that has been launched against these few can be compared only to the use of a nuclear missile when a peashooter would suffice.

Since the beginning of time, nature has grown plants without using chemical protection. The earth we inherited was covered with magnificent forests and verdant plains growing innumerable plants suited to their own particular environment. Entire areas were densely populated with a wide variety of plants growing side by side. That is truly nature's polycultural system. If, from the beginning of time, insects and disease had always attacked plants, as people believe they do, there would be no plant life left by now. Pests would have eaten everything and then died. Obviously modern agricultural thinking is following the wrong road.

The fine filaments of some fungi inhabiting the soil are almost invisible; the pulpy masses of others, such as mushrooms, grow on the earth's surface. A gourmet may balk at admitting that this exquisite delicacy is actually a parasite and a fungus, yet it is both.

An example of a "good guy" is the penicillium fungus, which was accidentally found to interfere with the growth of bacteria. An example of a "bad guy" is the fungus that attacks the human body, causing athlete's foot. Another "bad guy" is the common late blight fungus of potatoes that has, by destroying food crops and causing famine, forced people to migrate from one country to another.

Some bacteria in the soil are harmful to crops. Others are beneficial, acting on dead cells and converting them into substances that nourish plants. Still others fix atmospheric nitrogen for eventual use by plants, thus completing nature's cycle.

Any discussion of pests must include viruses, although it is difficult to be definite because scientists are still arguing about whether a virus is a living organism or not. We do know from bitter experience that viruses attack food plants, reduce yields and cause extensive losses. Viruses are transmitted from plant to plant and crop to crop when insects feed on a virus-infected plant and then move to healthy plants.

If a plant is infected with a virus, it may show symptoms of stunted growth, mottling and yellowing or crinkling of leaves. Most viruses cause only degeneration of the plant and reduce the yield.

Weeds are called pests when they interfere with the plants one is attempting to grow and when they compete with them for food, moisture and light. In other words, a weed is any plant growing in the wrong place. For example, when weeds are allowed to grow taller than cultivated plants, they shade the plants. This shading, even for a short time during the hot growing season, makes the plants less able to withstand the sudden shock of full sunlight when the weeds are removed. As a result, the growth of the plants is checked. Therefore, weeds must be removed before they have grown three-quarters as high as the plants.

When weeds do not compete with crops for light, moisture or plant nutrients, their role in soil regeneration is too valuable for them to be dismissed as pests. Weeds serve many useful purposes, and we should concentrate on harnessing them for our benefit rather than try to eliminate them. Deep-rooted weeds do the same important, soil-building jobs as cultivated plants. They bring minerals from deep in the soil and help the moisture rise by capillarity from the subsoil. Growers must consider how much time, energy and money should be spent in destroying what could be a useful ally. By covering the soil between plantings, weeds protect it from being leached by the rain and dehydrated by the sun and wind. Worked into the soil at the start of a new growing season, weeds increase the vital organic content of the soil.

Perennial weeds such as quack grass, with their strong root systems, also build up soil and bind it together. However, because of quack grass's special vigor (it will even grow through a potato), it cannot be tolerated in a cultivated area and should be eliminated before a crop is planted.

Before the advent of herbicides, there was a common expression: "The easiest time to kill weeds is before they can be seen." In earlier times, farmers had excellent techniques for weed control; unfortunately, these are slowly being lost with successive generations. Mulching, burying, tilling, raking and hand weeding are some of the effective methods of controlling weeds, and some must be used in combination.

For example, sod containing a good proportion of quack grass or other vigorous perennial weeds cannot be controlled satisfactorily by burying. In the old sod, most of the quack grass roots grow close to the soil surface under the natural grass mulch. If you are just working a small garden area, the sod, with a minimum of soil, could be cut off with a sharp shovel and placed in a pile to decay. Alternatively, a 6-inch (15-centimetre) layer of mulch, such as hay or sawdust, during a single growing season, will encourage the majority of roots to grow closer to the surface under the mulch, where they can be removed by hand. Sometimes it may be necessary to provide continuous cultivation until all the new shoots that are growing from pieces of root left in the soil are destroyed.

A crop planted late in the spring provides a longer period of preplanting cultivation and therefore offers more chance to clean the area before sowing seeds. Continuous removal of weeds as they appear during the growing period is still necessary to clean the area thoroughly so that they will not compete with the plants being grown.

Tilling the soil before seeding not only aerates and dries the soil but also has a stimulating effect on the weed seeds. These seeds may have been lying dormant in the soil for years waiting for suitable temperature, humidity and light for germination. This is one of the provisions nature has made for regenerating, covering and protecting soil in case of natural catastrophes such as flood, fire and landslides. There are almost always seeds where there is soil, ready to spring to life as soon as the germinating conditions are appropriate. Some require a long germinating period, whereas others take less time. In many cases, the latter appear through the soil before the seeds the gardener has so carefully sown.

Before the sown seeds come through the soil surface, the would-be gardener could be faced with a carpet of weeds, making it difficult to find the tiny seedlings of carrots, lettuce, beets or other vegetables. There are ways to efficiently control that preponderance of weeds, however. You will read about some methods in these pages and may develop some of your own.

To prepare soil in the spring, loosen it up to allow air in and at the same time break up the lumps. If lumps will not break up, the soil is either too wet or too dry. If it is too wet, allow time for it to dry—it may only take a day or two of fine weather. If the soil is too dry, either wait for rain or water it gently but not enough to make the surface water run. As the water soaks in, the lumps will soften and break up, provided the soil is not permitted to dry up again. Smooth the lumps and rake the soil level. Remove any of the larger pieces of vegetation that could interfere with cultivation. When the soil is smooth, make lines for the rows of seed. For depth of the seeds, see charts in chapter 8.

Make the furrows or lines very carefully to the correct depth, and shape the sides like a V so that the seed that drops into the furrow will tend to roll to the bottom. In this way, all the seeds will be at the same depth and in a straight line.

Here is a real work saver. At seeding time, mix a little radish seed with the carrots or beets or any other seeds you wish to sow. Thus, you will be sowing a mixture in the row and will accomplish several things: the plants will have the advantage of polyculture; the radish seeds will germinate first, outlining the rows of future seedlings in early stages; and the radishes will later provide you with a tasty spring treat.

As soon as you see the first line of radish just emerging, rake very lightly and carefully. Rake parallel to the lines of radish seed, not across the lines, and to a depth that might slightly disturb the growing radish seed. In two or three more days, remove one tooth from the center of the rake and carefully pull the rake along the radish row, but do not touch the radishes. You can work the rake fairly deeply into the soil but not so much that the earth will cover the row where the radishes are growing. Continue with this treatment and, as the seedlings grow, push the earth right up around their stems, making sure not to cover the leaves or damage them in any way. This will give you even better weed control because now you are covering weed seedlings right in the row. If you can keep this soil well up around the stems, you will have very few weeds and will observe the principal plants emerging. When the radishes are big enough, you may harvest them all and enjoy a spring treat comforted by the thought that you are harvesting your vegetables rather than just pulling weeds.

Keep a good watch for the germinating process of the seeds by looking for the first sign of the sprout. In most cases, it will show as a lighter-colored spot on the seed case from which the sprout will emerge. To watch for this, the grower must make special arrangements to be able to find the tiny seeds in the soil. At the time of seeding, choose part of one row and sow the seeds especially thickly so that they can be easily found. Mark each end of the thickly seeded part with sticks. Start checking the seeds four to five days after sowing for evidence of sprouting until the shoots emerge. Rake the soil above them a few times with the pre-emerge rake and you will destroy a great number of weeds, allowing the sown seeds to emerge relatively free of weeds. It may sound complicated and unusual, but many large potato growers have been using this type of weed control for many years.

On larger plots, much of this work can be done with a finely adjusted cultivator attached to a tractor. However, the inconsistency of some soils causes problems with this technique. The soil at Mylora, for example, was formed by the river. In some areas, it is sandy and soft, and in other areas it is dense clay, with all manner of variation between. The result is that the wheels of tractors sink into the softer soil, whereas they ride on the surface of a hard soil. This vertical movement means that a cultivator's teeth set to penetrate the soil to a depth of 2 inches (5 centimetres) may vary from 1 inch (2.5 centimetres) in the hard soil to 3 inches (7.5 centimetres) in the soft soil. When the teeth penetrate too deeply, too much soil is moved and thus the little seedlings may be buried. If the teeth are not deep enough, the cultivator does a very poor job in the harder ground.

At Mylora, we developed one fairly good, quick way to speed up hand weeding. A platform was fastened onto the back of the tractor and four people lay face down on it, with their arms hanging over the edge. The tractor was driven up and down the planted rows so that the platform covered four rows at a time, and each person weeded one row. Both hands were free to pull weeds, one hand on each side of the row. Our tractor did not travel slowly enough, so the results were not perfect. However, this technique was a vast improvement over getting

Mr. Harrison's octopus. The efficiency of each worker was increased many times by using the octopus.

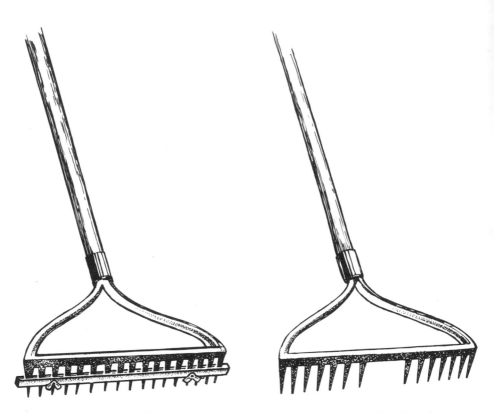

To rake the soil before the plants appear.

To rake the soil just after the plants appear.

down on hands and knees to pull the weeds in reach, then getting up and taking another step or two, then getting down on hands and knees again. We called the machine the octopus because eight hands did the weeding. Many new, efficient and much more comfortable machines have been developed especially for organic growers since those early days.

Weak plants attract insects. Research has shown that the weaker, defective plants that insects attack have higher carbohydrate contents than healthy plants, which have higher protein contents. Since insects have high energy needs, they look for high-carbohydrate-content plants; thus, they are attracted to weak plants rather than healthy plants.

Weather, too, affects the presence of insects. The weather may temporarily favor a speedy multiplication of pests and not their predators. For example, in our area we know that when the soil in the strawberry patch becomes too dry and the temperature too high, the mites multiply seemingly unchecked and damage the crop. This problem is solved by having an irrigation system ready to go into action during dry spells. You can test this phenomenon yourself. Leave a few plants dry and watch the insects come. Then water the plants in a few days and the insects will leave.

Organic growers must never allow themselves to depend on any harmful form of pest control. It is sometimes tempting, when you are desperate and when you want to cooperate with the regional control program, to make a temporary pact with the devil. A short-term success can weaken your resolution, and you may put yourself in danger of becoming dependent on chemicals and finish in the same situation as chemical farmers.

Pesticides destroy only some pests and allow others to flourish because they create an ecological imbalance. Target pests may not receive the dose required to kill them, especially if they are sheltered by leaves or foliage, or they may absorb only enough of the chemical to acquire resistance to it. Others may have more natural resistance and will not succumb to the material used. These two circumstances can result in the breeding of offspring with even greater resistance, requiring more and more powerful chemicals to combat them.

Even if a pesticide is 100 percent effective in eliminating the pest of the moment, the break in the chain of life exacts a payment in succeeding seasons of growth. The natural predators that would normally feed on the now-destroyed pest either perish for lack of food or move on to other areas. The following year there is little or no natural predator control. So artificial control becomes necessary, and the mad spiral accelerates with little or no assessment of the complications and damage left in its wake.

In 1945, only 13 kinds of pests were found to be resistant to the pesticides then available. Forty-five years later, over 500 types of pests had developed a resistance. Today there are on the market over 50,000 commercial products manufactured to combat resistant pests. Pesticides have helped to create this menace, and their continued use only perpetuates the development of super pests. This attempt to dominate nature has proved to be not only regressive but also ineffective. As many as 40 years ago, the U.S. Department of Agriculture stated: "Never before have so many pests with such a wide range of habits and characteristics increased to injurious levels following the application of any one material as has occurred following the use of DDT in apple spray programs." Therefore, our only alternative, which is an alternative for survival, is to cooperate and live harmoniously with nature.

Some scientists estimate that far less than 1 percent of the pesticides used actually hit the target pests and that of the remaining 99 percent some adhere to the plant surface to provide protection against pests but most are discharged into the atmosphere to cause colossal and unnecessary environmental damage.

Pesticides washed out of the soil and into the waterways continue to wreak havoc with the marine life they encounter. Such damaging effects stop at neither targets nor boundaries, and their lethal qualities are increased by a process known as biological magnification. In this process, one of the lower forms of life consumes or absorbs some pesticide, which is then concentrated in a specific part of its body. When this insect pest is eaten by its predator, the concentration of the pesticide in the predator becomes intensified because of the number of prey consumed. This procedure continues up the biological ladder, with each successive and larger predator acquiring a more and more concentrated dose of the chemical. The ultimate consumer is eventually treated to a massive dose.

Herbicides are chemicals that destroy vegetation. The range of herbicides available today makes it possible to destroy all vegetation in a given area or to select one herbicide that, it is claimed, will destroy most of the weeds in a crop and leave the food crop apparently unharmed. Unfortunately, there is no scientific evidence that this food crop is unharmed.

These selective herbicides dramatically reduce the cost of weeding crops such as carrots or onions, particularly in areas of high rainfall, where weed seeds germinate continuously throughout the growing season. Hand weeding small seeded crops such as carrots, for example, could cost ten times as much as using herbicides during a wet spring. It is not difficult to see why organically grown, chemical-free crops are more expensive, in the short run, than those treated with herbicides. Even though the cost of herbicides to the farmer is small, the resulting expense to the community is great because, like pesticides, their capacity for destruction—of both the environment and people—extends far beyond the field in which they are used. Herbicides have the awful capacity to change the genetic pattern of some living organisms, including humans.

The chemical industry has made available to farmers an arsenal of modern pesticides and herbicides that are without a doubt very effective in killing. In order to build sales and profits, these chemical companies have employed the talents of specialists in merchandising, marketing and advertising. At the receiving end of this massive brainwashing is the ultimate buyer of the farmer's produce—consumers. Trained by years of multicolor, glossy magazine illustrations to judge food by its appearance rather than by how nourishing it is, they refuse to buy food that does not look like the magazine illustrations. Wholesalers and retailers in turn refuse produce that does not have this "plastic" quality. Growers are compelled to make certain that there are neither insects nor insect damage on the food they send to market.

The very acceptance of the term "health food store" speaks volumes about the safety and nutrition of the food distributed and sold in all other stores. No one denies that much of our food contains lethal pesticides. We generally accept this on the understanding that these foods are supposed to contain only "safe" amounts of injurious chemicals, which are supposed to be strictly regulated by government for the protection of our physical health and not for the financial health of the manufacturers. However, the ingestion of even "safe" amounts of poison from food, whose only real function is to promote life, health and nourishment, is a blatant contradiction. Why are we not all revolted by this situation? How can anyone guarantee that no more than the so-called safe amount remains on any food? How can we be sure that no lethal or genetically damaging or environmentally destructive residues remain on the food when it reaches the dining table?

Washing food removes only what is on the skin; it fails to remove any material taken up by the plant as it grows. The pesticides can become a part of the plant. How can pesticide residue be effectively monitored when, for instance, a carrot may contain one or more of the many different commonly used pesticides? Different pesticides, different farm locations, different crops, under different circumstances—all of these would require a testing program that would be astronomically expensive and time-consuming. The general public really has no choice other than to accept food offered for sale, trusting that it will not contain too much pesticide.

Unfortunately, pesticides may accumulate in our bodies and injure us years later or affect our genetic cells and produce mutations in our children, our grandchildren and our great-grandchildren. Were the earth to have a large-scale pesticide disaster, millions of people could be victimized. The final price is more than we can afford to pay. We have only to remember the Bhopal pesticide disaster.

Obviously a pesticide disaster must not be allowed to happen, yet we continue to put massive chemical dosages on food plants. Pesticides have not been around long enough for us to know the full effects of ingestion during a human lifetime. Nor can we know their full impact on subsequent human generations because there has not yet been one complete generation, let alone the several necessary to ensure that no damage has occurred.

Fortunately, ecologists and environmentalists are increasingly active. They must put the natural fertility of the soil and the nutritional quality of the food the soil produces at the top of their priority list. The prime motive in growing food must be to provide the highest nutrition for the consumer, not merely to produce a food free from poison. Therefore, the grower must understand the importance of working in accord with the laws of nature. If growers operate in this way, the ecological system not only will be sound and sustainable but also will improve the health and fertility of the soil for the long-term betterment of the whole world. Arguments for this statement are extremely clear and powerfully written by the original organic farming experts, Howard, McCarrison and Balfour, and others.

Among the pest problems we encountered and controlled at Mylora were Red Stele in strawberries, aphids in dill weed, green cabbage worms, club root in cabbage, crane flies in grass, rust fly in carrots, and the flea beetles, aphids and scab that took their toll on potatoes in various seasons. Through the years spent puzzling, investigating and experimenting, we suffered our share of failures, but successes occurred often enough to encourage further efforts. They were often dramatic enough to convince us that we were on the right road to finding permanent solutions to our problems. For instance, once we had learned how to grow dill without inviting an aphid attack and had identified and corrected the biological error that drew carrot rust flies to our crop, we solved these particular problems for all time. No more worrying, puzzling or losing crops.

In contrast, most commercial growers approach the pest problem in a completely different way. Growers have been conditioned to believe that the only good aphid is a dead aphid, so their solution is to obtain the most effective aphicide available. Although that works for the first season, three questions remain unanswered:

How much of the potent spray used remains on the harvested food to be ingested by human beings?

If the aphicide destroyed only the weaker strain of aphid, how powerful a chemical will have to be used in subsequent years to control the stronger, resistant members of the species that were not destroyed?

What further difficulties will both the predator and the prey of the offending aphid cause in the immediate or distant future?

Another problem with the indiscriminate use of pesticides is that it upsets the prey-predator relationship. It interferes with the biological balance between organisms that injure the plants and the insects that control these organisms. Upsetting this balance opens the door to new outbreaks of insect pests and disease.

Applied biological control is the process of introducing predators, such as the lady bug and praying mantis, to eat the insects that threaten a crop. One of the dramatic successes using the predator method of control was the importation from Australia of the Vedalia beetle to wage biological warfare on the cottony-cushion scale that was threatening to destroy citrus crops in California. When the enemy pest was routed, the cost of this safe, effective and natural control method was found to be a mere five thousand dollars. Sterilization of males of the pest species is still another method of biological pest control. It has been used successfully to control screw worms among herds of livestock. The total cost of biological insect control is far, far less than that of chemical control.

Applied biological control has two disadvantages, however. First, should a second pest for which there is no biological control appear on the scene and require chemical control, the predators applied to control the first pest could be harmed by the chemical. Second, the organism introduced to control the original problem can sometimes create a new problem of its own.

Still, since applied biological control involves the use of materials and organisms that are not destructive to the environment, its use is much preferable to chemical control. In unusual circumstances—for example, in forests, rangelands or non-food-producing areas or when a pest is accidentally imported into an area that lacks its natural predator—biological pest control appears to be an ideal solution. Nevertheless, we do not know the long-term effects of biological control. In commercial agriculture, it is preferable to use sound organic practices and to maintain a natural environment that harbors predator-type insects.

Winter, the slack time in the grower's calendar, is the time for organic growers to consider pest-control techniques for the coming season based on successes and failures during the previous season. However serious or trivial a pest problem, its very existence indicates that one or more biological errors have been made. The following questions will aid in identifying the source(s) of the problem:

1. Was the soil adequately drained the previous winter?
2. Was the soil properly prepared and adequately nourished?
3. Were the seeds or tubers planted viable and of good quality?
4. Were the seeds planted at the right time of the year?
5. Was the area planted polyculturally, with no single species so large that the planting was monocultural?
6. Was a place provided where beneficial predators could survive during their dormant period?
7. If such an area was provided, was it close enough to the growing area for the predator to reach its prey?
8. If any species of plant was infested by pests, was that species of plant suitable to the area?

Converts to organic growing may underestimate the rate at which they can assist nature in soil-building. Organic material, provided it is well rotted, can be added to the soil at any convenient time throughout the year, although it will take usually more than one season to produce healthy, living soil.

Until such a soil is established, the incidence of insect and disease pests in crops is apt to be unpredictable. If one particular crop attracts more pests than others, it would be wise to abandon growing that crop until the soil enrichment program has had a chance to work. If, however, economic necessity dictates a repeat planting of the previous year's troublesome crop, the farmer faces a difficult decision—either use natural but admittedly safe materials and salvage what can only be inferior plants, or lose a large percentage of the crop to the same pests or diseases that attacked the year before.

The serious organic grower will choose to assign the difficult-to-grow plants to those areas with the healthiest soil conditions and will first set out small blocks of plants among dissimilar plants. There really is no reason to plant a crop that is continually attacked by disease or insects other than to attempt to cash in on some high-money crop. To do this is to adhere to the faulty premise that food is just another commodity. But food is not just another commodity; it is a necessity, the staff of life. It is like a public utility, and it therefore must be treated as such. However, farmers must no longer be victimized. Their future must be guaranteed; otherwise, their children will not remain on the farm.

The garden hose can be an effective insect control when it is used knowledgeably. Lack of moisture can so weaken a plant that it will attract insects. An adequate supply of moisture makes the plant healthy, so it grows at its optimum rate and insects will not be attracted to it. This very simple solution seems too easy to be credible to many, but moisture distribution has been constantly stressed in these pages because it is at the very core of successful organic growing.

Another method of repelling insect pests is by planting strongly aromatic herbs, such as sage, thyme or rosemary, among food crops. Flowers such as marigolds or nasturtiums, either by their fragrance or symbiotic relationships at the root level, serve the same purpose.

Some enthusiasts place much emphasis on companion planting, mostly, I think, because of its exotic appeal. Certain plants do benefit one another, however, and others tend to depress each other. Books on companion planting are available, containing lists of both types of plants, beneficial and depressive.

I know from experience, however, that insects attack plants that are not growing at their optimum rate. The problem can be prevented if you provide all the plants' needs. Although I do mention safe remedies to control insect pests, once again I must emphasize that polyculture provides most of the answer. Add to this correct seeding and planting in a truly living and fertile soil.

We experimented in polyculture by planting alternate rows of beets and cabbages and were richly rewarded with the vigorous growth of both vegetables. The beets did especially well, and a comparison with another field in which the beets were grown monoculturally showed that the tops of the beets grown among the cabbages were markedly superior. Although we cannot answer the questions about the protein-to-carbohydrate ratio or the mineral content, the flavor test indicated good quality. We are still wondering whether this success was related to the symbiotic factor or to sunlight. In polyculture, the taller-growing plants receive the full sunlight on the upper surfaces of their leaves and the upper part of the stem only. The lower part of the stem, as well as the soil at the base of the stem, is shaded by the lower-growing plants. In our experiment, the lower-growing plants, the beets, received their sunlight filtered through the leaves of the taller cabbage plants. Previously we believed that food plants must have all the sunlight possible on every part of their foliage. Now we wonder.

Organic growers must be patient and curious observers of nature. You may be tempted, in desperation, to resort to chemicals, but it pays in the long run to go with Mother Nature.

Chapter Seven
Planning Your Garden

Mixed farming is the secret of success, no
matter how much it complicates the managerial
function.

Sir George Stapledon

After this exploration of the basic principles of organic
cultivation, I hope you are ready, with packages of seeds in hand, to
put these principles into operation in a single season. Such motivation
and enthusiasm are required to change the destructive course of
conventional chemical agriculture. But before you tear open the seed
packets, you should recognize that the vestiges of poisons used in the
past make intelligent planning essential. And you must recognize that
it will take longer than a single season of sanity to correct soil
imbalances and to restore the natural cycles to your property. But the
excitement, the triumphs and the amassing of knowledge of your own
land during a single growing season will make each step toward natural
cultivation immensely satisfying.

Whether you have an acreage or a garden plot, you must plan well
in advance of planting time. The best time to make your plan is in
the winter. It helps to actually draw your plan on paper.

One of the first steps that will pay off handsomely is to completely
investigate and explore your area. Learn from your neighbors what their
experiences have been in growing different crops. Find out what diseases

and pests they have encountered through the years. Luckily, farmers and gardeners are far more willing to recount their experiences and secrets than are cooks to disclose their favorite recipes. Even if your growing principles don't match those of your neighbors, there is a lot to be learned from their experiences. News of the latest super-poison will be of no value, but you may have to find protection from its intrusion onto your soil if it is widely used in the community. The good will of your neighbors is most important when you request that spraying be done at a time when the wind will not drift the spray onto your garden. If the water from adjoining areas naturally seeps onto your land, you can alleviate or avert a problem by digging a drainage ditch to carry the water away.

Decisions about where particular plants should be placed are best made after knowledge of prevailing winds, previous winter conditions and present soil conditions are ascertained.

Given a choice of a gardening site, always choose one with a slight downward slope to the south. The least desirable is one that dips downward to the north. Too steep an incline permits the soil to dry out too rapidly, although it does have the advantage of warming up somewhat earlier in the spring. Before any decision is made to change the contours of the land, it is wise to weigh these factors along with the requirements of the crops planned for it. The organic grower must always take into consideration the fact that radical changes in contours will upset the tiers of the organisms in the soil and will require special attention until that balance can be restored.

All is not lost if the garden site faces due north. Heat-loving crops such as corn, beans, tomatoes, squash and cucumbers may have to be bypassed, but the hardier types, such as carrots, beets, parsnips, peas, lettuce, green onions and cabbage, can all be expected to thrive in fertile, living soil. Even in the most depressing growing conditions, a devoted gardener can produce miracles by adding generous quantities of well-decayed organic materials.

Do not use all your land merely because it is available. It is far better to grow fewer vegetables that offer superior nutrition than great quantities of poor-quality fare. Set aside unused land to be built up by adding organic waste material in preparation for subsequent growing seasons, or plant soil-improving crops such as rye, vetch or clover to refurbish the organic content of the soil. If areas are kept mowed, they present a neat appearance and weeds will not go to seed. In effect, such fallow fields may be said to be increasing their own fertility. When such an area is needed for gardening operations in the future, this growth need only be cut up and worked into the top of the soil to complete its restorative cycle.

Choose suitable types of vegetables for your family's taste and make a realistic assessment of the amount of food you will need from your garden. Plan for less rather than more so that you can give your garden adequate care.

The question of how much to plant of each food crop is determined by your preferences and the projected yield of the land available for planting. I offer the following rough guide to the maximum yield that you can expect from one-eighth of an acre (0.05 hectare) of a good crop, approximately 20 yards by 30 yards (18 metres by 27 metres), based on our experience at Mylora: strawberries, raspberries, peas, beans and broccoli will yield approximately 1,000 pounds (454 kilograms); cucumbers, cabbages and beets, about 2,000 pounds (907 kilograms); potatoes, squash, turnips or onions, about 3,000 pounds (1360 kilograms). Carrots and tomatoes should definitely yield at least 5,000 pounds (2268 kilograms).

It is often a temptation for the learning gardener to choose the new, different or unusual plants so attractively displayed in the seed catalogue. But it is wiser to postpone such experiments until you have enough experience to assess their special requirements. A great number of them are hybrids and are only a few generations away from the experimental stage. It takes time to determine if they will thrive under a system of organic culture. In all probability the new breed will depend on chemical fertilizer—the quick fix.

Many new varieties of plants may not be satisfactory for organic culture because seed producers cater to commercial growers, their largest customers. Breeding plants with characteristics that such customers require can result in the loss of vigor. These will be of little use to the organic farmer whose aim is to have vigorous plants for maximum nutrition. For instance, commercial food processors may demand a variety with the ability to undergo the processes necessary for their particular form of preservation. At the same time, retailers may seek a strain that will maintain an appearance of health for a long period of time after the vegetable is first displayed for sale. They must reach their optimum growth with the aid of chemical fertilizers and pesticides from the moment of planting. Such plants may not do well in organic gardens, since their special characteristics may have been gained at the expense of vigor.

Since many of these varieties have qualities that interested our customers, we experimented with some of them at Mylora. We tried very hard with a number of varieties to grow small pickling cucumbers, but were unsuccessful in producing vigorous plants with a satisfactory yield. Yet large table or slicing cucumbers thrive in the same field. It appears that plant vigor had been lost in the development of the small pickling varieties we attempted to grow.

So stay with the tried and true varieties unless you have information from an experienced person that a new variety has proven to be satisfactory over some years. Since seed catalogues and packages do not always identify which varieties have been developed for their commercial qualities, it is difficult to find the well-established strains. However, many of the newer varieties have initials or numbers in the plant names indicating that they are newcomers and may have been bred for particular commercial qualities.

Planning for every growing season includes ensuring that the soil is well nourished. Sheet composting is a method of soil enrichment that involves layering organic materials one upon another. Ideally, the materials for this purpose are specially grown plants (such as rye or vetch) that are incorporated into the soil instead of being harvested, properly prepared compost, well-rotted manure and fresh manure, in that order.

The ideal time for sheet composting is when freshly planted rye (or other soil improvement plant) is about 6 inches (15 centimetres) high; at this stage, the plants will provide some protection for the organisms in the manure and can easily be lightly harrowed. Compost or well-rotted manure can be applied fairly heavily, although about 10 percent of the soil surface should still remain visible. Fresh manure should be limited to a thin coating. Covering the manure lightly with soil, using a rake, hoe or harrow, will prevent drying out, which would damage the organisms in the manure. The greatest value of the manure or compost is in the living organisms it contains.

If you use fresh manure alone, leave about 50 percent of the surface uncovered for a light application, and 25 percent uncovered for a medium application. The manure will be worked on by soil organisms and will offer a better source of plant nourishment when planting time arrives. If you apply fresh manure to the soil just before planting root crops, the unseasoned manure will tend to cause irregularly shaped roots.

The best times to apply compost are in the spring, immediately after the frost is out of the ground and the soil is dry enough to work, and in the fall, after the crops are harvested but the weather is still not cold. At these times of year, considerable moisture from night dew and rain showers will provide good conditions for sheet composting.

Once you have developed a system for achieving fertility, you will have no need to bring in manure, since the vast number of soil organisms will be continuously producing manure for your plants and the green manure crops you will be growing between your vegetables will in time also increase the organic material for your soil. When the soil has achieved a high degree of fertility and the surface is constantly protected, your gardening will become easier.

In addition to the sheet composting method, which we used for many years at Mylora, there is another popular method, the compost box method, which was developed by Sir Albert Howard.

If you use this method, you will need to construct a box, fastened together with bolts so that it can be dismantled, about 4 feet by 4 feet (1.2 metres by 1.2 metres) and 3 feet (1 metre) high. Coat the wood with a natural preservative, such as linseed oil, to lengthen its life. The sides of the box must be slatted to allow free air access. No bottom is necessary, since the compost must come into direct contact with fertile soil—not with sod—to facilitate the interaction between the organisms already present in the soil and the new compost you are preparing.

When you put the daily waste—such as vegetable gratings, eggshells and fruit rinds—into the box, sprinkle some dry soil over the surface. A pile of loose, dry soil protected from the rain should be kept handy for this purpose. The soil assists composting and prevents odors. When a 6-inch (15-centimetre) layer of waste has accumulated, add a 2-inch layer of manure to provide the activity for composting.

While building the pile, keep the material loose by gently forking the top layer with each addition. Do not press down on the pile. A stout, upright stick should be placed in the middle of the box during the building. When the box is full, remove the stick and leave the hole open to provide ventilation. The pile must be protected from sun, rain and wind to prevent it from becoming too moist or too dry. The moisture content must be continuously maintained to the consistency of a wrung-out sponge. In warm, dry weather, the pile may need a frequent light sprinkling with a watering can.

Should the pile become smelly or attract flies, it could be too wet or too dry, and the material should be remixed. If the box is almost full, it may be easier to unbolt the box and move it slightly, then repile the materials, adjusting the moisture content.

When the box is filled to the top, unbolt it and set it up elsewhere to begin a new pile. Cover the existing compost pile and allow it to ripen until it is friable, or easily crumbled, and sweet smelling. The time this takes varies according to the weather. If the compost is repiled after cooling down, the ripening process is accelerated. Some gardeners work with two compost boxes.

If the compost cannot be spread as soon as it is ripe, cover it with a film of plastic until it is needed. When the compost is spread over the garden, it must be raked or forked into the soil immediately. This should be done on a cool, damp day or in the evening so that the compost does not dry out.

If you do not have the space or the inclination to build your own compost box, there are compost-making containers on the market, with full instructions, that are suitable for the city dweller. There are basically two types of these containers. The better type allows adequate air for bacteria to produce an excellent woodsy-smelling compost. Those compost-making containers without adequate provision for the access of air and for turning the compost are not desirable.

Finally, there are biodynamic methods of composting, which produce excellent compost for the exacting gardener; they are not for the average gardener or farmer. The methods are complex and detailed, and I do not think that the average gardener would use them. Most gardeners prefer one of the simpler methods described here.

As a soil conditioner to lighten and enrich heavy clay soils, sand is an inexpensive and most valuable commodity. Sand is a storehouse of minerals, which nature has wisely locked up in a form that is insoluble in water. Were this not so, the minerals would all be washed away and wasted. We have already seen that plants are the only agents that can change the inorganic soil minerals into organic minerals and thus put them into the cycle of life. Every time that sand is moved, either for transportation or to be applied to the soil, there is friction between the particles. This friction exposes some of the previously oxidized surface of the particles, and as a result this fresh, exposed surface is more vulnerable to the searching plant roots and provides them with a more accessible source of the mineral nutrients.

Probably the most difficult and challenging task facing the gardener is that of preparing to grow a garden on an old sod-grass area that has been undisturbed for a number of years. It can tax the body as well as the mind unless a rototiller is available to cut the sod into fine pieces. Even so, it may take two or more treatments to cut the pieces finely enough to make a workable soil. To those who must attack the sod with only a sharp spade, it becomes a temptation to cut out large squares of sod and bury them beneath the topsoil. However, we know this is biologically most undesirable. It is better to remove the top layer of sod, pile it up and leave it for a season, or compost it and then return it to the soil when it is decayed. Sod pieces that are cut up and not removed almost certainly will grow again, and if you remove them by pulling them out after you have planted your crop, you may also uproot small seedlings such as onions or carrots. If the area must be planted before the sod is broken down to a fine, workable tilth, it is advisable to plant larger-seeded vegetables, which will not pull out as easily when pieces of sod are removed. Potatoes are the usual crop to follow sod, but beans, peas or corn could also be grown.

Sod that has been rototilled must be allowed to dry before it is worked any further. Soil is dry enough when a lump of it breaks and crumbles into pieces under pressure of the foot or hand; if it squeezes into a smaller lump, it is too moist. Working a clay soil when it is too wet produces hard lumps that are difficult to break up when dry. Sandy soils can be worked earlier in the season but require greater amounts of organic material to combat their sievelike texture, as well as more irrigation in the warmer weather.

When the topsoil has been loosened up and is moderately dry, the condition of the subsoil should be checked to make sure it is porous and loose enough to allow roots, air and water to penetrate. If it is found to be too compacted, the topsoil must be removed, the subsoil broken up and then the topsoil replaced. Take care to ensure that the respective layers are returned to their original position so that there is as little disruption to the life in the soil as possible. For large farms, tractor-drawn implements are available. When pulled through the soil, they hardly disturb the topsoil but thoroughly loosen the subsoil.

Before seeding begins, the surface tilth must be correct, because it can mean the difference between success and failure. The organic farmer uses the size of the seed to be planted as a rough guide for the size of the soil particles. These must be fine enough to cover the seed completely and consequently exclude atmospheric air from coming in contact with the seed. Making the seedbed finer than necessary merely because it is eye-pleasing is not only a waste of effort but unnecessarily destructive to the soil. It must be remembered that once soil structure is destroyed, the transference of moisture to the plant is restricted.

Just as burying sod beneath the topsoil is biologically unsound, so is burying such garden trash as clippings, leaves and other dead vegetation. These errors seriously impede the natural processes of the soil in making plant food for growth. When undecayed material is buried, it acts as a sponge, preventing the movement of moisture from the subsoil to the surface and drawing the moisture from the topsoil downwards. The effect, then, is to provide a drying agent rather than a feeding system during the growing season. Furthermore, the bacteria living in the airless soil below this spongy mat and working without oxygen break down the organic material into an inferior plant food. The resulting material has a most objectionable odor. Ideal plant food smells woodsy and sweet.

Therefore, lay down this undecayed material when it is fine enough as a mulch over the surface soil, and it will be acted upon by the bacteria at the surface, which can extract from it the nourishment needed for plant life. This is the natural method of recycling dead vegetation, and it is the method nature has used in building the soil.

Even after the seed bed is fine enough to begin planting, it pays to wait a week or two to give weeds a chance to germinate. Tilling done to prepare the soil for seeding brings dormant weed seeds into germination, and even though these tiny seedlings are invisible, they are there. One fine raking before seeding kills many of the weeds and saves a great deal of effort later in the season, thus validating the adage that the time to kill weeds is before you see them. A two-week delay in planting time means little more than a few days delayed harvest, for the plants grow more rapidly with later, warmer weather.

Do not confuse the organic term "biological balance" with pH level, which is the measure of acidity of the soil. As organic farmers, however, we regard pH readings of the soil as purely academic. We know from experience that well-drained soil that is being nourished with organic material grows healthy, vigorous plants. What more does one need to know?

For the curious, the range of pH readings related to ordinary vegetable growing conditions is in the range 4 to 8. A reading of 7 indicates a neutral soil; any reading above 7 indicates alkalinity, and below 7 acidity. Most vegetable crops grow in acidic soils. Lime is one of the materials suggested to neutralize acidic soils, but we used no lime on our fields at Mylora for over twenty years and still our crops flourished. If we had joined the pH crowd with the litmus paper tests, there is no knowing how much money and time we would have wasted in trying to attain artificially what we accomplished through the natural recycling of organic materials. In contrast, chemical farmers, having applied chemical fertilizer regularly, can have a buildup of acidity in their soils. They must, therefore, use lime to counteract a problem of their own making. I remember an old English saying: "Lime and lime and still more lime makes poor farms poor and poor farmers poorer and poorer." It is a fact that adding lime can cause soil deficiencies of various elements such as boron, iron and manganese. Even though these minerals are present in the soil, there can be a chemical reaction between lime and the mineral itself, causing the mineral to be held in an insoluble form because of the presence of lime.

Here is a list of general rules to follow when you are preparing the soil for your garden:
1. Do not interfere with natural drainage—just make it more effective.
2. Prepare the soil as early as possible, preferably in the fall.
3. If necessary, open the subsoil for air, water and root penetration.
4. Do not invert the soil. The upper layer of top soil belongs on the surface and the lower layers belong below. If you do have to invert it to break it up, then you must re-invert it before planting.
5. Add all the good compost and/or well-rotted manure you can.
6. Do not work the soil when it is wet. It must be dry enough to break up easily. If it is a clay soil, do not even walk on it when it is wet.

Chapter Eight
Planting and Growing

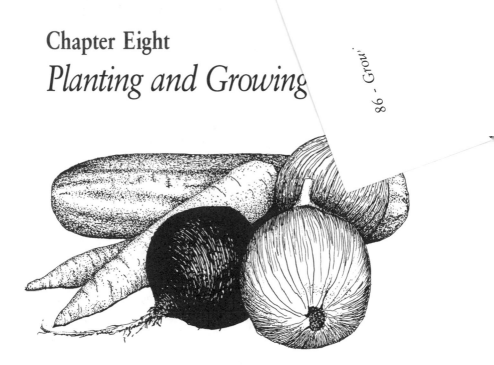

Good—Better—Best
Never let it rest,
Till your good is better
And your better, best.

This little inspirational verse was molded into the steel plates at the back of the horse-drawn Furfy water cart and must be emblazoned on the mind of every Australian farmer who ever carried water to thirsty animals. It is good advice for the convert to organic cultivation as well.

One summer, as a result of many requests arising from the numerous talks I had given to various groups interested in organic farming during the previous ten years, we set aside part of Mylora for teaching organic growing methods to about 120 enthusiasts. I had given a course during the school year that covered the basic principles of organic growing, and it was mainly the students from this course who participated in our first "on farm" practical program. Plots of organically prepared soil, 20 feet by 25 feet (6 metres by 7.6 metres), were measured out for each of the 60 participating couples, and the aim was to provide the normal vegetable requirements for a family of four for the summer months from each of the plots. This goal was accomplished most satisfactorily. Mylora contracted to provide seeds and plants for a dozen easy-to-grow vegetables, along with the necessary tools. We also prepared the soil for planting, and I gave weekly instructions on the growing phases as the season progressed.

The experience of learning and working together was an enriching one for all of us. Our very diversity—there were professionals, artists, tradespeople, students, homemakers and reporters—enlivened our discussions. There was just as wide a range of gardening experiences. Some had gardened for years using chemical fertilizers and pest control, and others had never planted a seed before.

Sometimes students preferred to do things their own way, providing further learning experiences for all of us. I remember one student who had seeded his carrots too thickly. They needed thinning, but the weather had been wet, and the soil was too wet to walk on without damage. Nevertheless, the student went ahead and thinned his carrots out that day because he was going out of town for a week. When he returned, all his carrots seemed to be growing nicely. We then had a spell of warm weather, and suddenly his carrots began to look sickly. Further examination revealed carrot rust fly damage. The soil, which had been too wet, had been packed by the weight of his feet, excluding air from the soil around the roots. This damage to the soil had caused the plants to become sickly and thus attract pests. None of the other students had any problem with their carrots.

Another student was carefully planting tomatoes, but instead of taking the moist soil from a slightly greater depth to cover the roots, he chose the easier route and took it mostly from the drier surface soil. For a week or two all the tomatoes were fine, but soon everyone else's tomatoes started to outgrow his. His plants never really recovered, and he harvested fewer tomatoes as a result. These experiences provided an excellent lesson for the whole class.

An evaluation of the project at the end of the summer showed that an average of only two hours of work twice a week was required on each of the plots for the students to learn how to grow and harvest enough vegetables for a family of four. The initial preparation of the soil had been done by the Mylora crew, so planting, weeding and harvesting constituted the students' main chores. Many planned to plant some of the more difficult species during the next growing season. The knowledge that 120 more converts to nutritious, poison-free food and a cleaner environment had taken their basic training in the organically treated soil at Mylora has been a source of deep, personal satisfaction to me.

Number of Plantings

This chapter gives instructions for three plantings that provide continuous harvests throughout the season. Instructions for an extra planting, which you may want to include in your second year of organic growing, are also given.

Each planting is designed to take advantage of the symbiotic relationships between different families of plants and is restricted to plants that are relatively easy to grow. More temperamental crops that are particularly attractive to insects and disease have been left out.

Times of Planting

Timing is always a critical factor in obtaining optimum germination. The dates set out in the planting charts in this chapter are predicated on our experience at Mylora, which is located on the 49th parallel of latitude, at sea level, and is well protected from prevailing winds. Another area, which might be located in a hollow or on a windy hilltop, will require an adjustment of several days from our own dates. If you are not confident of your planting dates, it is always wise to ask an experienced gardener in your area for safe planting times.

Even in a comparatively small holding such as Mylora, we observed dramatic differences in timing. Bisected by a north-south freeway, Mylora had an eastern half and a western half. The western fields lay between the freeway and a housing subdivision, whereas the eastern half was quite open, with only a few houses scattered on the periphery. We learned that strawberries planted in the more sheltered plot west of the freeway ripened three days ahead of those growing in the more exposed eastern fields. We also experienced spotty damage in tomatoes caused by unseasonable July frosts in those eastern fields.

Tools

The following is a suggested list of tools for working your plot.
Garden rake
Hoe with a 7-inch (18-centimetre) blade
Garden hose and sprinkler
Pointed-nose shovel
D-handled garden spade
Garden fork
Sticks and string for marking
Wheelbarrow
Manure fork

For a large garden, you also need to rent or buy a rototiller. A combination hand seed planter with attachments for cultivating also expedites the work.

Seeding

Buy seeds in bulk whenever you can. First, buying seeds in attractive packages is usually more expensive than buying in bulk. Second, it is difficult to estimate the number of seeds in a sealed seed package.

If you have any seeds remaining from the previous year, sow them more thickly, since the percentage of seeds that germinate diminishes with time. Some gardeners add the old seed to the new and plant this mixture a little more thickly.

The three main factors that determine the planting depth are the size of the seed, the time of the year it is to be planted and the moisture present in the soil at the time the seed is introduced. The depths indicated on the planting charts apply to Mylora soil, which varies but is mostly a medium clay and very cold in a wet spring. You must also bear in mind these three facts:

1. A tiny seed cannot push through too much soil.
2. The seed must not dry out during the germination process.
3. During warmer weather, the soil dries out from the top down.

The measurements given in the charts are those we used, and they were quite satisfactory. However, they are merely a guide for the novice gardener. Some plants thrived anywhere at Mylora, but we learned that certain species, such as carrots, beans and raspberries, grow considerably better in light soil. The majority, however, including strawberries, potatoes, broadbeans, beets, parsnips and tomatoes, prefer heavy soil. Peas, corn, squash, lettuce and onions grew equally well in our heavy or light soil.

To help you assess your soil, here are some guidelines. Heavy soil weighs considerably more than light soil, as you might have guessed. Furthermore, particles of heavy soil tend to stick together more than light soil; these sticky particles form hard lumps of soil that do not break up easily. Light soil is warmer, dark in color, loose and friable and will run through your fingers even when damp. Usually the heavy soil is cooler and light in color.

The Garden Plan

This is a plan for 850 square feet (80 square metres) of planted garden. The suggested twenty-three rows with 15- to 22-inch (38- to 56-centimetre) spacings shown in Figure 2 require a width and length of approximately 42 by 20 feet (13 by 6 metres).

In the teaching allotments, we used 12- and 18-inch (30- and 46-cm) spacings between rows. Although these spacings were adequate for the

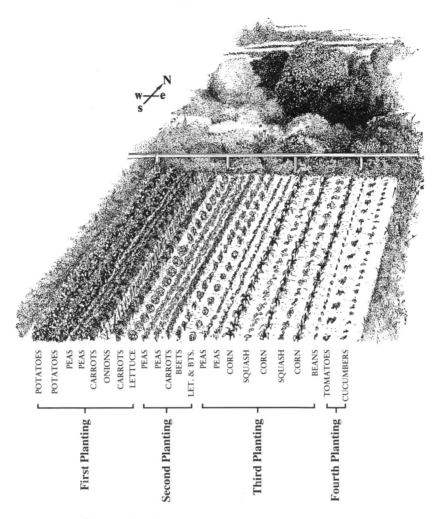

POTATOES
POTATOES
PEAS
PEAS
CARROTS
ONIONS
CARROTS
LETTUCE
PEAS
PEAS
CARROTS
BEETS
LET. & BTS.
PEAS
PEAS
CORN
SQUASH
CORN
SQUASH
CORN
BEANS
TOMATOES
CUCUMBERS

First Planting

Second Planting

Third Planting

Fourth Planting

Diagram 2. The Garden Plan.

smaller plants such as carrots, they were a little close for inexperienced gardeners to work with, and so we suggest a wider spacing here. Closer spacings are recommended in subsequent plantings.

The First Planting

If you have never planted fine seeds before, it is worth your while to practice doing so. Take a pinch of seeds between the thumb and first two fingers. By moving the thumb slightly, practice dropping them onto a surface from which they can be easily recovered, such as a table with a soft cloth on it (otherwise seeds will bounce or move out of the position in which they fall). Practice until you feel you have control over their fall and the seeds are distributed evenly.

Try to choose a calm day for seeding, since a breeze will blow and scatter the finer seeds. It should not be raining, yet the soil should be moist and worked to an appropriately fine tilth. Also, when seeding in dry weather, make sure that the seeds all fall into the moist soil. The time between opening the furrow and covering seeds should be as short as possible, so as to conserve the precious moisture.

On the day of seeding:

1. Make a straight line parallel to the north-south boundary of the garden. A string stretched between two sticks in the soil provides a satisfactory guide.
2. With the handle of the hoe, make a furrow along the line of the string at the depth suggested for the seed to be sown (see Chart A). Once the furrow is opened, the seed should be sown and covered up immediately. The seed should then be lightly tamped down with the back of the rake so that the earth touches the seed and prevents it from drying out.

A. First Planting

Crop	Minimum Depth of seed	Space between mature plants	Distance to next row	Expected planting time	Time of emergence in weeks
Potatoes (whole seed)	1½" (4 cm)	10" (25 cm)	22" (56 cm)	April 15	3-4
Peas	1" (2.5 cm)	½" (1 cm)	15" (38 cm)	April 15	2¾-3
Carrots	½" (1 cm)	½" (1 cm)	15" (38 cm)	April 15	2¾-3
Onions	½" (1 cm)	½" (1 cm)	15" (38 cm)	April 15	2¾-4
Lettuce	¼" (0.5 cm)	6" (15 cm)	15" (38 cm)	April 15	1½-2½

Notes:

1. Lettuce: We suggest half a row of leaf lettuce and half a row of head lettuce. The variation in the times necessary for maturity will spread out the harvesting time, giving you a continuous supply of lettuce over a longer period.
2. Peas: Space the peas carefully. They are better not thinned out. Plant them in adjacent rows and encourage them to become entwined with one another so they do not fall on the neighboring rows of other plants. Hill up adjacent rows of peas so that they fall towards each other.

We found that the extra labor involved in tying and staking the tall-growing peas is too costly, so we used only the dwarf varieties of peas. The pea plants occupy more space than if they were trained to grow up some fishnet or mesh wire, but they require far less work.

3. Potatoes: Very small whole potatoes can be used for the first planting. After the potatoes are planted, the soil should be hilled over the row about 2 inches (5 centimetres) above the general soil level.

4. Before dropping the seed in the furrow, consult the chart again for the distance required between the plants when they are fully grown. You will need to plant more seeds than the number of mature plants you will eventually need, since not all seeds germinate. We suggest three or four times the number of fine seeds such as those of lettuce, carrots and onions. Plants will push one another apart as they grow.

When fine seeds fall in a cluster, they are hard to thin after they germinate. To keep fine seeds from clustering, mix them with a little fine soil and scatter this mixture in the furrow. If the seeds have already accidentally dropped into the furrow in a thick mass, you will find it difficult to recover them, so mix them well with the soil on the bottom of the furrow and scatter this mixture along the line about as thickly as you were sowing them.

Crowded seedlings will be spindly, since they are competing with one another for soil moisture and light. Furthermore, the thinning-out process is apt to damage those left behind, so a careful sowing and spacing saves future headaches.

Broadbeans need 8 to 12 inches (20 to 30 centimetres) between plants. Peas, beets, carrots, onions and parsnips grow to a good size if spaced 1 to 2 inches (3 to 5 centimetres) apart. If the root vegetable seeds are spaced too closely, the developing vegetables will compete for space and push on each other. Green onions, however, can be spaced closely, half an inch (1 centimetre) apart in a double or triple row, since bulb development is less important than a large green top. Keep in mind that spacing of plants is determined by the size the mature plants will attain, although wet growing conditions may require even wider spacing.

A gardener using conventional monocultural growing methods has to be especially careful not to space plants too closely, since their uniform height reduces air circulation and encourages such problems as fungus diseases. The organic method of polyculture, with various types of plants growing adjacent to one another, has fewer problems with air circulation and plants can be placed closer together, thus yielding a greater total quantity of food.

5. Cover the seeds to the correct depth according to the charts. Carrots, onions, lettuce, parsnips and parsley may be planted in a shallow furrow with just enough soil to cover them completely. This thin layer of soil helps the seeds maintain moisture and protects them from birds that could eat them and heavy rains that might wash them out of position.

6. Rake the surface above the seeds lightly and gently until it is smooth and free of lumps. Hold the handle of the rake vertically so that the tines rest on the soil surface. Pat the soil gently all along the surface of the seed furrow with the flat of the tines.

7. Proceed until you have the whole row completed, then consult the chart for the space between the rows and go to the next row.

8. Mark the rows of seeds with named tags. Immediately prepare and smooth an additional garden area for the second planting (see Chart B, page 94) to encourage germination of weed seeds in that area. Again, wait for the next germination of weeds before you do the final raking.

Consult Chart A for the approximate time the seedlings will emerge. Do not walk on any planted area until you can see the rows of emerging seedlings. You will then know just where to place your feet as you work the soil. You may have difficulty distinguishing vegetables from weeds that emerge at the same time. However, the straight rows of planted seedlings can be relied on to show the location of the rows. You can then hoe the area between them.

Potato plants take longer than most vegetables to come through the soil surface. Pull the soil up over the tops of the rows of potatoes, using soil from between the rows. After a week or so, the hilled-up soil can be raked down but not leveled completely. The whole operation can be repeated two or three times, and it provides a most effective weed-control system. If, during these rakings, you remove all the soil from the top of the row, you may have difficulty in finding that row again for subsequent hillings. In larger plots, be sure to keep the tractor wheels in the right place. If you do not take care at this early stage, some of the potatoes could be pulled out before they have come through the soil, and even if they are replaced immediately, their growth will be severely retarded.

At the time the foliage of the plants is emerging, the soil should be as level as possible. When the potatoes are well up and growing vigorously, the rows can then be hilled up again. This time the soil will be around the stems of the growing plants with the soil again sloping away from the plants; the worst weeding days then are over. Subsequent rains could start another crop of weeds germinating, but, with the soil hilled up around the plants, the water runs down the slope without wetting it enough to stimulate more weed germination. This water may germinate weeds in the low areas between the rows, but a fast hoe job eliminates their claim to the soil nutrients. It could be preferable to leave them alone.

The rains may cause a hard, dry crust to form on the soil surface, which depresses the plant so that it attracts flea beetles. These insects lay their eggs at the base of the potato plants, and when the eggs hatch, the larvae burrow down into the soil and feast on the growing potatoes. Nature, as we have commented earlier, covers the soil and keeps it aerated and of a consistent tilth. Crusted soil is an unnatural condition; therefore, it follows that soil not protected by a cover must be hoed to keep it loose and friable.

Once plants have reached the stage where their foliage shades the soil, weeds fade out of the competition for light, moisture and nourishment and are no longer the threat that they were when the plants were quite small. In fact, weeds now become allies in the march toward a triumphant harvest. This change in attitude toward weeds, from regarding them as unrelenting enemies to inviting them as symbiotic partners, often proves difficult for new organic growers to accept.

The first spring plantings of hardy vegetables are not harmed by normal spring frosts, but they can be damaged by heavy rains that either wash seedlings out of position or, in the case of clay soil, pack the ground and thus prevent air from circulating through the soil. Germinating peas are very sensitive to the resulting muddy soil conditions, which do not allow any air around the seeds, and they can quickly succumb to fungus infection and decay. Compacting of topsoil is never healthy or helpful for plant life, so gentle hoeing after the soil dries is required following any pounding downpour.

The Second Planting

A reliable indicator that we used for timing the second planting is that satisfying spring day when the rows of the first planting show the green line of seedlings. Lettuce usually shows up first, about eight to ten days after planting. Onions follow in another four or five days. Carrots may take as long as three weeks from the seeding date until they emerge.

As Chart B indicates, the second planting should be sown around May 1. Although all the charts are based on mathematical calculations, soil temperature is the governing factor. Thus, if the weather is very warm or unusually cold, adjust the date accordingly.

In this planting, some of the same types of plants sown in the first planting are sown again along with some new types of plants.

B. Second Planting

Crop	Minimum depth of seed	Space between mature plants	Distance to next row	Planting time
Peas	1½-2½" (4.0-6.5 cm)	¼" (0.5 cm)	15" (38 cm)	May 1
Carrots	¼" (0.5 cm)	¾" (2 cm)	15" (38 cm)	May 1
Beets	¾" (2 cm)	½" (1 cm)	15" (38 cm)	May 1
Lettuce	½" (1 cm)	10" (25 cm)	15" (38 cm)	May 1
Potatoes	2½" (6.5 cm)	10" (25 cm)	18" (46 cm)	May 1

Note: For this planting we suggest a half row of beets and a half row of head lettuce.

Since the soil will be warmer and drier at the time of the second planting, the seeds must be planted somewhat deeper than the earlier seeding. In this way, they will be completely surrounded by moist soil, ensuring proper germination. Because the soil temperature is higher, germination should occur more rapidly. The soil over this second planting must be pressed down a little more firmly to keep the moisture close to the surface, particularly through the sprouting period. To do this, gently tap the soil over the seeds with the back of the rake immediately after sowing them.

Beets

With beets, as with lettuce, a high moisture content in the soil is an absolute necessity for effective germination. If the soil seems overly dry, mix some of the deeper, moist soil with the surface soil at the time of planting. I suggest this method rather than adding water, since only the top couple of inches may be dry, whereas there could be an adequate supply of moisture just below the dry area. Adding water might only chill the soil unnecessarily. Deeper soil unfortunately brings with it not only moisture but new weed seeds as well. The organic grower takes a philosophical and practical view of this mixed blessing and considers that it is far better to have weeds growing with beets and lettuce than not to have weeds or beets or lettuce. Another method of overcoming surface dryness at planting time is to dig a deeper planting furrow right into the moist soil layer, deposit the seeds, and top them with just enough moist soil to cover them. Be careful not to bury the seeds the full depth of the furrow or they may never emerge. When the seedlings have grown high enough, level the soil.

Potatoes

Now is also the time to plant winter potatoes. For the second and subsequent plantings use medium-sized potatoes cut into chunky pieces with at least two eyes left in each piece. The eye is the small indentation in the surface of the potato from which the sprout will grow. Chunky pieces rather than slivers of potatoes are preferred because the cut area is vulnerable to disease, and the smaller the cut area, the quicker the surfaces will dry and the better the chance of successful germination. Seed potatoes should be cut several weeks ahead of planting time and thoroughly dusted with hydrated lime, and the pieces should be stored where there is good air circulation. If the ground dries and warms up early in the season, potatoes can be cut immediately before planting. This is a gamble, however, since a return of cool, wet weather makes them susceptible to fungus infections and other diseases.

Thus far we have used only vegetables in our illustrations of the practical application of organic principles. However, with the increasing concern over poisonous sprays, questionable food additives and nutritional deficiencies in the food offered in the marketplace, many readers may wish to grow all their food free from such contamination. Organic farming methods will bring to your table as wide an array of flavorful and nourishing foods as you could want. Perhaps you have suffered indigestion when you have eaten chemically grown onions or cabbages; this problem usually results not from the vegetables themselves but from the chemicals used to grow them. You may discover that you can really enjoy eating such vegetables when they are organically grown. Over the years, many of our customers have told us that they were able to eat and enjoy our onions and cabbages without suffering unpleasant after-effects, whereas they were unable to eat those bought from regular stores without unpleasant consequences.

Herbs

At Mylora we planted chives, mint, horseradish root and garlic cloves early in April, and sage, thyme, dill, rosemary, sweet basil and summer savory in May. Mint has a vigorous root system that rapidly spreads over wide areas, so plant it in an isolated area or, better still, in a pot. A cylinder sunk around the plant about 18 inches (46 centimetres) deep confines the roots. Herbs like a sunny spot but do not need rich soil. If the soil is very rich, the growth will be vigorous, but lush growth does not have the aromatic quality of slower-growing plants. When herbs are planted beside the garden path, they grow out over the walk, where their leaves are crushed underfoot, giving you the pleasure of their fragrance in the garden air.

Cereals

For centuries, cereals have proved invaluable in sustaining entire nations, and they still do. The overrefined sugar-coated forms touted by modern merchandisers are a pale imitation of the robust, flavorful grains in their natural state. Millet grain was once almost the exclusive diet of generations of people in large areas of China, whereas rice has been the prime staple of most of the rest of Asia. In Scotland, oats have played an important role. For food value alone, cereals rate a high priority as subsistence foods. They have the added advantage of being easier to store than root vegetables, with a much longer storage life. You will discover how good bread can be when you bake it from your own organically grown wheat, freshly ground in your own kitchen and formed into the aromatic, taste-tantalizing loaves that should not even have to share the same name as the air-filled, doughy concoctions sold in the stores. If you sprout whole wheat for two to three days and add the sprouted grain to the dough, the amount of nutrients is greatly increased. (See chapter 10 for more about sprouting.)

Cereals should be planted with the second group of seeds in your planting schedule and should present no problems if the soil is healthy. Good news for porridge lovers is the variety of oats that has no coarse hull overcoat and thus does not require hulling. When oats are mechanically hulled, nutrients are lost.

Weeding and Thinning

When the soil is prepared for the third seeding, and the second seeding is complete, you can begin weeding the first planting. These instructions apply to almost all vegetables except potatoes. The method for weeding and hilling potatoes is outlined later.

You must be able to distinguish the emerging seedlings from the weeds. Because the first two leaves of a seedling sometimes have

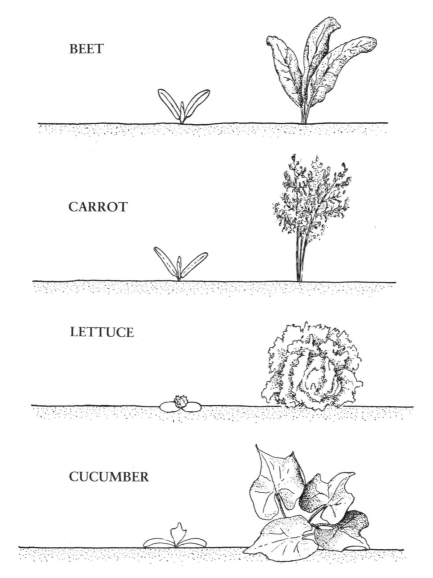

Diagram 3. Identifying Seedlings.

characteristics that differ from all subsequent leaves, it is wise not to weed or thin out a row until you are absolutely certain that you can differentiate between the seedlings just planted and the unwelcome weeds. Diagram 3 should help. When in doubt, wait until the seedlings have produced at least four leaves and have developed their definite characteristics. As soon as you are sure, remove all the weeds.

When weeds that you did not remove the first time because they were too small to see have grown about three-quarters as high as the vegetables, it is time for the second weeding and first thinning. Thin the plants, leaving twice as many as needed; then, should you damage some of the young plants, there are enough remaining to provide a good crop. The vegetable seedlings you pull out on the next thinning will be large enough to eat. Be sure, however, that the final thinning is done before the leaves of adjacent plants begin to crowd one another.

After the second thinning and weeding, pull the soil gently up and around the stems of almost all the plants by hand or by using a hoe. Some of the lower leaves of the plants may be covered with a little soil, but those on top must always remain exposed to the sunlight. This process is called hilling, and it encourages the plant roots to invade the very rich area that was formerly surface soil and has just now been covered. Hilling also smothers tiny weed seedlings, which may germinate close to the stems of the plants and would otherwise be difficult to remove. Both beets and lettuce should be hilled only very lightly, whereas onions must not be hilled at all or they will develop thick necks. If some onions do grow thick necks, use them first, since they will not keep as well as the others.

As soon as the soil is prepared for the third seeding, the soil that has been hilled up over the potatoes from the first seeding (see Chart A) should be carefully leveled with the rake. Explore the newly uncovered soil with your fingers, looking for sprouts from the potato seeds, and observe and note their length. Be careful not to break the sprouts or disturb the seed. Remake the hill again in exactly the same place. If you are not exact in remaking the hill, you may inadvertently damage some potato sprouts.

Repeat the process about every five days until the sprouts are long enough to emerge through the level soil. Do not remake the hill but leave the soil level. The hilling and raking should control weeds.

When the potato plants are 6 to 9 inches (15 to 20 centimetres) tall, they can be well hilled up.

The Third Planting

After the second seeding is completed, prepare the rest of the garden needed for the third seeding, as in Chart C on this page. This third planting will include the heat-loving vegetables—corn, beans, squash, tomatoes and cucumbers. We would begin to plant them at Mylora around the middle of May. We found it advantageous to plant each kind at about two-day intervals to ensure a continuous supply of fresh, young vegetables. A two-day difference at planting time in the hot summer can make a difference of a week or more at fall harvest.

C. Third Planting

Crop	Minimum depth of seed	Space between mature plants	Distance to next row	Planting time
Peas	1½" (4 cm)	½" (1 cm)	15" (38 cm)	May 15
Corn	1½" (4 cm)	10" (25 cm)	22" (56 cm)	May 15
Squash	1½" (4 cm)	10" (25 cm)	22" (56 cm)	May 15
Beans	1½" (4 cm)	1" (2.5 cm)	15" (38 cm)	May 15
Tomatoes-use plants	cover roots adequately	22" (56 cm)	22" (56 cm)	May 22
Beets	1½" (4 cm)	1" (2.5 cm)	15" (38 cm)	May 30
Cucumbers	1½" (4 cm)	6" (15 cm)	22" (56 cm)	May 30

Note: Three-quarters of a row of green beans and one-quarter of a row of golden butter beans provides a delightful variety.

Beans

Beans of the small bush varieties can be planted now and will be ready to harvest before the weather becomes too cold. Beans that require poles for support need a longer growing season than bush varieties and need more labor, so we changed over almost completely to bush beans. The exception is the Romano or Italian bean. Because of its tenderness and flavor, we decided that this pole type is well worth the extra labor involved in growing it. The pod is larger, longer and somewhat flatter than most commercial varieties and so tender that the beans fall apart even if they are slightly overcooked. This fragility makes the Romano type unsuitable for the commercial processors, so the gardener will find that the seed is difficult to obtain because of small demand. There is a real need for devotees of natural foods to rescue these fragile varieties from extinction by growing seed for themselves and other discriminating gardeners.

Spring Peas

Planting peas to follow the spring harvesting is practical providing that an early-maturing variety is chosen. These varieties generally withstand foggy fall weather with the attendant mildew problems much better than most of the later-maturing types.

Radishes

Radishes are a short-season crop and can be planted almost anytime. Unless the soil is in very good condition, however, insects such as flea beetles and root maggots are apt to be a problem.

Tomatoes

Tomatoes are usually grown from plants rather than from seeds. In our northern climate, yield depends on the number of frost-free days. While the weather is still cool, tomatoes are started in a heated greenhouse so that they are well-established plants by the time the threat of frost has passed and they can be set out in the garden. It is important that tomato plants be purchased from a reputable grower and that they be delivered in the same box in which they were grown in the greenhouse so that the buyer can be sure the roots have not been disturbed and are therefore undamaged. The two main types of tomatoes are (1) the tall vine type, which must be staked and tied and knowledgeably pruned at regular intervals and is the hardier of the two, and (2) the short vine bush that requires neither staking nor pruning but is less hardy. The latter requires slightly warmer weather before transplanting. These bush varieties are our favorites.

Mylora tomatoes were planted between May 20 and 24. Even on the hottest day we were completely successful with the following transplanting technique: About four hours before the transplanting is to take place, the lawn sprinklers are turned on so that they just mist the tomato plants, which are still undisturbed in their cartons. The sprinkling continues for the entire planting period. A very slight depression is made in the row where the tomatoes are to be planted. The soil in the carton is cut into sections so that the roots of each plant are cut out rather than pulled out when the plants are removed from the carton. Each plant is then eased from the carton with an undisturbed cube of soil around the roots and laid horizontally in a furrow that is just deep enough to cover the complete root cube to a depth of at least half an inch. The plants must be handled carefully so that no soil falls from the cubes and the soil is not compressed. Particular care must be taken to ensure that the roots of the plants are neither damaged nor exposed to the sun or wind for longer than it takes to remove them from the carton, place them in their position on the soil and cover them. All the plants must be laid horizontally in the same direction so that the person weeding the tomatoes will know on which side of the upright stem the roots are and therefore will not damage them with the hoe. Cover the roots and about half of the stem with fine, moist soil, firming it with a gentle pressure. The stem must be left lying horizontally, not turned up. If the surface soil is dry, push it away and take the moist soil from a deeper layer to cover the roots. Be careful not to break the roots by pressing too heavily. Within a few days, the growing tip will have turned to a vertical position and normal growth will continue again. Do not forget when hoeing around the plants that the roots are on one side of the upright stem, not below it.

When the plant is placed horizontally against the soil surface, it is kept warmer along its entire length, since the surface of the earth absorbs heat during the day and radiates it back at night. The roots are stimulated by this heat to reach through the surface and begin to work downward in search of food. Extra roots grow from the part of the stem that is covered. Instead of suffering traumatic shock from the transplanting process, the plants hardly know that they have been moved, and in a very little time ripe tomatoes are available. Most growers dig a hole deep enough to cover all the root cube plus an inch (2 centimetres) or so of the stem. This hole can easily attain a depth of 6 inches (15 centimetres) or more. At that level the soil is cold, and since the plants have come from a warm greenhouse they suffer shock and frequently change to a blue or purple color.

Beets

Examine the beet seed carefully and observe that it resembles a piece of cork. In each seed there may be two or three individual seeds, making a cluster. You can see this if you break open the cluster. Naturally, planting one whole cluster will give you two or three seedlings. Commercial growers have the clusters put through a process in which the "cork" is broken so that the individual seeds are freed. The cork protects the seed from moisture, so adequate soil moisture is necessary for its best germination.

If germination is irregular, it is in all probability because of lack of moisture. It would be wise to give the soil a good soaking before seeding. Should irrigation be deemed necessary, we found at Mylora that it is far better to apply the water after the top residues of the previous crops have been removed and before the soil is worked. Water falling on an undisturbed dry soil surface readily percolates into the soil through root and worm holes and cracks. In contrast, water falling on finely worked soil tends to seal the surface of the loose earth and then runs to the lower spots, leaving higher areas as moisture deficient as before, while the lower areas are oversaturated and stay wet too long. Moisture must be distributed evenly for successful seed germination.

Corn

Corn needs some attention to ensure a bountiful harvest. Shoots that appear on the lower part of the corn stems develop into small cobs, most of them incompletely pollinated. If they are removed, the plant matures earlier and grows slightly larger cobs. At this time also, corn plants need a final hilling with soil, which must be piled up carefully around the stems so as not to damage the roots. The purpose of this final hilling is to check the last lot of weeds and at the same time give the roots a better chance to anchor themselves in the soil. This anchoring helps the plants to stand upright even when they are growing in a soft, friable soil and are weighed down with heavy, rain-soaked cobs. It is worth the effort, for if the stalks collapse before the cobs mature, the kernels will not develop fully.

Timing

Time is of the essence in summer seeding operations. Irrigated soil dries out very rapidly, especially while it is being worked. The soil is best left alone during the heat of the day and cultivated in the cool of evening. It is imperative that the seeds be planted as soon as the soil is in a sufficiently fine state of tilth. When seeds are planted in dry weather, the soil must be pressed down firmly enough so that no air passages are left between the seed and the surface through which soil moisture can escape. This is most important.

We usually seed peas, beans and carrots until the middle of July, whereas broccoli, beets and lettuce can be successfully planted any time through the end of July. Once August has arrived, the planting season has ended for all practical purposes—only a few vegetables, such as Chinese cabbage, broccoli and radishes, can be planted after the end of July in our area.

The latest dates on which we seeded the various kinds of vegetables are given in the list below:

Final planting dates	Crops
June 15	Mid-season corn, cauliflower
June 15	Early cabbage, early peas
July 1	Carrots, broccoli
July 15	Green and wax bush beans, green onions
Aug. 1	Head lettuce
Aug. 15	Leaf lettuce
Sept. 1	Chinese cabbage

Extra Planting

In your second year, you may wish to try some of the crops that can be more difficult to grow (see Chart D). Parsley, for example, takes a long time to germinate and the soil may dry out. It will help if you place some old sacks or other light material over the seeded area. Watch for the emergence of the seedlings and remove the cover as soon as you see them. Never uncover them in the heat of the day.

D. Extra Planting

Crop	Minimum depth of seed	Space between mature plants	Distance to next row	Planting time
Broadbeans	2½" (6.5 cm)	15" (38 cm)	22" (56 cm)	Late March
Parsley	½" (1.25 cm)	8" (20 cm)	15" (38 cm)	Early April
Wheat	1" (2.5 cm)	½" (1 cm)	6" (15 cm)	May 1-10
Oats	¾" (2 cm)	½" (1 cm)	6" (15 cm)	May 1-10
Parsnips	1" (2.5 cm)	1" (2.5 cm)	15" (38 cm)	May 20
Early Cabbage	1" (2.5 cm)	12" (30 cm)	15" (38 cm)	May 20
Late Red Cabbage	1" (2.5 cm)	22" (56 cm)	22" (56 cm)	May 20
Savoy Cabbage	1" (2.5 cm)	22" (56 cm)	22" (56 cm)	May 20
Early Broccoli	1" (2.5 cm)	22" (56 cm)	22" (56 cm)	May 20
Late Cauliflower	1" (2.5 cm)	22" (56 cm)	22" (56 cm)	May 20
Late Broccoli	1" (2.5 cm)	22" (56 cm)	22" (56 cm)	June 1
Swede Turnips	1" (2.5 cm)	4" (10 cm)	12" (38 cm)	June 1
Chinese Cabbage	1" (2.5 cm)	6" (15 cm)	12" (38 cm)	Late August
Fall Rye	1½" (4 cm)	½" (1.25 cm)	6" (15 cm)	Early September

Those plants that mature in cooler weather, such as cabbage, broccoli and cauliflower, can be seeded between May 20 and 25. Turnips should not be planted until the end of May. Usually cabbage, cauliflower and broccoli are transplanted into the garden, having been started in a nursery bed. Many years' experience firmly convinced us that the check in growth caused by transplanting can be enough to weaken the plants. Consequently, they attract insects, particularly flea beetles, but aphids and root maggots are also on the lookout for weakened plants of these species.

During this period of adjustment to their new locale, the young plants do not grow at their optimum rate. We therefore rejected transplanting and instead planted seeds of these varieties directly in the garden in their permanent positions. Sow them more thickly than needed and thin them out later. Be sure to completely remove these thinnings. Dying cabbage plants lying on the soil surface can attract insects.

Broccoli and cabbage need watching during hot weather since the all-important soil moisture becomes depleted and insects may then attack. Irrigation remedies the situation, providing there is no club root disease in the area. The spores of this fungus attack members of the cabbage family. A combination of saturated soil and high temperature encourages the fungus spores to germinate. To prevent such an attack, it is wiser to merely moisten foliage and the top of the soil frequently and wait for a drop in temperature before using full irrigation.

Small Fruits

Strawberries

Strawberries are a tricky crop. They vary considerably in their growth patterns from one area to another, so it is helpful to find an experienced grower among your neighbors who can tell you what to expect. Reserve the richest part of the garden for strawberries, and be sure it is well drained. In the Pacific Northwest, strawberries spend the first year developing in order to produce fruit in the following season.

A good-sized plant with a number of crowns (the central woody stem part of the plant between the roots and the leaves) may be developed. Alternatively, many small runner plants could be encouraged. If the former, place the plants 12 to 15 inches (30 to 38 centimetres) apart and cut off the runner plants as fast as they develop. If you want many runners instead, space the plants 40 inches (100 centimetres) apart and encourage the runners to take root by arranging them carefully and anchoring them in place with some soil so they can develop roots as they run. Whichever method is used, removing the blossoms during the first year will strengthen and encourage the plant to survive the dangerous winter ahead and set an adequate amount of fruit the following season.

Unfortunately, strawberries sometimes fail to survive the winter because of freezing, suffocation from too much water, or infection by root diseases. They may be eaten by mice or moles, which also appear to have a craving for the crowns of the plants. Another winter hazard to strawberry plants is the height of the water table. This should not be closer to the soil surface than 18 inches (46 centimetres).

If you are concerned because of the high winter mortality rate of strawberry plants, you can use new varieties that fruit late in July immediately following planting. They do not have the full-blown flavor of the standard variety, but at least you will have some crop to justify your efforts before the plants face winterkill. If you are lucky and the plants survive the winter, you will have some berries in the following spring as well.

The precautions we took at Mylora against the Red Stele organism were to plant the strawberries in the richest soil available. We removed all the runners and ensured adequate drainage because poor drainage is a major cause of Red Stele proliferation. We also grew over twenty-five different varieties in an attempt to overcome Red Stele. We recommend that you contact your department of agriculture or a reputable plant grower for information about suitable varieties.

To plant, use only good plants, preferably those dug during dormancy and held in cold storage until planting time. When the soil is thoroughly warm, transplant them, spacing plants 12 to 15 inches (30 to 38 centimetres) apart.

Only the extreme top of the crown and the leaves—if any—should remain exposed to the sunlight after planting. The roots should be straight and well fanned out in the soil. The soil must be made unusually firm around the roots. We suggest May 8 as a good planting time.

Remove blossoms as they develop, keep the weeds checked, and remove the runners as they appear, or anchor them, whichever method you prefer. At the end of the summer, see that the drainage ditch surrounding the fields is about 18 inches (46 centimetres) deep.

Raspberries

Canes should be purchased from a reputable grower and should be set out in the spring. A spacing of 2.5 to 3 feet (0.8 to 1 metre) between plants in the row is usual, and as in all planting and transplanting, extreme care must be taken to tamp the earth firmly over the roots so as to exclude all air. Set the canes in the soil so that their former rooting area (all the parts of the roots that were in the ground) is completely covered. Maintain a dust mulch and check the growth of weeds.

In the early spring after the first year, a number of new canes will have grown. Remove all the old canes down to the soil level. One year later you will have a still-greater number of new canes. Again remove all the old canes and leave six to ten of the thickest of the new canes per plant. You will also need to support these canes with twine on a fence or trellis, whichever is available.

Watering

The best time for watering the garden is in the early morning. The soil will then have a chance to warm up after being chilled by the water, and the leaves can dry off during the heat of the day. Evening waterings of such crops as potatoes or beans encourage the development of fungus diseases by prolonging the moisture on both surface soil and plant leaves.

Soils vary in the rate at which they can absorb moisture, so apply the water at no greater rate than the soil can absorb it. If too much is applied, the soil becomes packed and water runs to the low spots, carrying some of the topsoil with it.

Sometimes it takes as long as twenty-four hours for moisture to become thoroughly dispersed throughout the soil. Therefore, allow this much time to elapse before adding more water. Make sure that there is not a layer of dry soil between the newly moistened surface soil and the moisture in the lower part of the topsoil; otherwise the surface moisture will rapidly evaporate. You can check this condition by digging into the soil with your hand. When the surface has dried after irrigation, loosen it with a hoe and make a dust mulch to conserve the moisture you have just applied.

Watch the moisture content of soil during hot, dry weather. Coarse, sandy soils dry out much more rapidly than fine, clay soils, and insect attacks can result.

Cover Crops

The organic grower must always ensure that the soil surface has enough protection during the winter. Late June is the time to start planting soil-improvement crops for winter protection and soil enrichment. Unless other crops are planned for this time, the garden can be worked up and vetch, fall rye or clover can be seeded. The rye will be fairly tall by fall, so it can be worked into the soil at the end of August, the garden can be reseeded, and there is still time for another seeding of rye to grow for soil protection during the winter.

The advantage of rye is that it grows all winter and makes

considerable top growth as well as even more root growth. An experiment was performed with a single plant of rye, which was grown in 2 cubic feet (0.05 cubic metre) of soil for a single season. If the roots of this plant were laid in a straight line, they would have extended a distance of well over 300 miles (480 kilometres).

It is obvious how much top growth is produced when one realizes that one plant can have six or more stalks, each about 4 feet (1.25 metres) long. Thus the total yield of organic matter from one seed in one growing period is outstanding.

In mid-July, clover can be seeded among the vegetable crops. This practice is called underseeding. A common method is to scatter the seeds over the plants while they are growing. The seeds will eventually fall to the soil below and germinate when conditions are suitable. Clover seeds can also be seeded by hand through crops that are to be harvested later in the fall or by hand immediately before the last hoeing and soil cultivation. This action mixes the seed with the soil for better germination. If the seeding is not done before the last cultivation, germination will not be very good, unless the weather turns wet quite early.

An alternative is to encourage the growth of weeds. Sometimes small weeds may be showing growth at this time and can be encouraged if you cut the tops of the neighboring taller plants so that the sun can get at the weed growth. The soil will be covered even faster by weeds than by a planted crop, provided the weeds are thick enough on the soil surface.

Water Drainage

The ideal way to ensure soil drainage is to contour the soil so that water naturally runs off the surface. First take the soil from the outside of the field or garden, from walkways or from where a tractor turns, and place this soil in the lower areas to make the entire surface slope very slightly to the outside. Make sure that seed beds are 30 inches (76 centimetres) wide and about 4 inches (10 centimetres) higher than any walkways. The walkways must all be interconnected and all should lead to the drainage canal and away from the garden plot. Although it is generally not a good idea to displace soil, a minor disruption for something like soil drainage is sometimes necessary.

Winter Preparation

Before the garden is left to the vagaries of winter, a survey of

drainage spots is essential. If low spots cannot be filled
way or other area where the loss of soil is inconsequential,
rovide a drainage channel to the main ditch. Never allow
water to collect and lie stagnant on any part of food-producing land.

When we first started farming we made an understandable but costly
mistake in an attempt to solve a drainage problem in one of Mylora's
fields that was quite uneven. To overcome the difficulties associated
with low spots, we hired a bulldozer to move soil from the tops of the
high spots and push it into the low areas until we had a level field.
We were assured by growers who were using the same technique, but
whose results had not been tested by time, that any damage to the soil
would repair itself quickly. However, the massive dislocation of soil
and soil organisms turned this field into a continuing problem. It was
always the focal point for insect pests, disease and disappointing crop
yields, no matter what crop was planted. Only after the passage of
many years and the application of countless loads of manure did the
soil scars disappear and healthy, luxuriant crops prove that the soil
had, at last, come back to full organic life.

On other fields, we removed topsoil from the outside edges of the
fields and the areas that served as roadways and turnabouts and
deposited it in the low spots, using the method described above. Thus
a field was leveled and natural drainage provided. This method had
the added advantage of being permanent. Where the water table is not
too high, this method is far superior to installing permanent tile or
wooden underdrains under the fields. The water that tiles collect has
to be pumped out, requiring expensive equipment and services, and
sometimes the tiles become blocked and cease to function effectively.

Our system required no maintenance and drained free water away
slowly. Without the usual underdrains, the water table during the
growing season was higher for a longer period, and thus more moisture
was available to maturing plants during the critical growing season,
and the cost was minimal.

Rules for Planting and Tending Your Garden

Here are some general rules to follow in planting and tending your
garden:

1. Do not rush the planting season. Give yourself time to kill the
   many weeds that germinate as a result of cultivating your field.
2. Set out plants or sow seeds at the appropriate time. That is, seed
   early-maturing varieties early and late-maturing varieties late.

3. Make certain that seeds are not sown too thickly. Remember that every extra seed should be removed by hand. It is quite tedious and unnecessary and can be avoided by taking extra care initially.

4. Thin the seedlings as early as possible, preferably not in the heat of the day. Thinnings of many vegetables can be used in salads. If you don't eat them, bury them or use them in compost, especially members of the cabbage family. Dying vegetables are particularly attractive to insects.

5. Remove weeds before they are three-quarters the height of the plants. Maintain a dust layer on the surface to conserve soil moisture or cover the soil with hay straw or other such material.

6. Observe your plants continually and maintain enough moisture at the root level.

7. Do not cut or damage plant roots with a hoe or cultivator when working the soil.

8. Do not cultivate too deeply. Keep the dust layer on the surface very shallow.

9. Maintain a protective layer of vegetation on soil surfaces as constantly as possible.

10. Always provide hospitable conditions for predator insects—they will repay you. Encouraging heavy, natural vegetation around sides and edges of the garden helps insect control by providing protection for predator insects.

11. Do not use synthetic plant foods or chemicals such as fungicides, herbicides, nematocides or soil sterilants. Remember you are dealing with living soil. Put nothing lethal or chemical on the living soil.

12. When insects or diseases threaten, think how you may have caused the conditions that drew them. Is your soil in good condition? Have you observed all the *dos* and *don'ts*? For example, if little black beetles are eating the very young cabbage plants, ask yourself, "Did I start the seeds in a nurse bed, or did I buy them already started and then shock them by transplanting them?" This situation applies particularly to all the cabbage plant family.

13. Water your plants, particularly in hot weather. They suffer stress if there is not enough moisture, and then they can attract pests such as aphids, flea beetles and mites.

Chapter Nine
Harvesting and Storing

*It is everybody's business to realize that what
the farmer grows today will be their bodies and
their bodies' health and strength, tomorrow.*

Sir Cedric Stanton Hicks, M.D.

Flavor and the Time of Picking

Like all organic growers, I regard flavor as a guide to the nutritive value of food. It is really nature's hallmark of quality after all—flavor and aroma determine which plants herbivores will eat. Full flavor is only present when the plant has had all its requirements satisfied, and these include hours of sunshine and degree of heat as well as nutrients from the soil. Lack of full flavor indicates nutritional deficiency, which the plant passes on to the consumer.

Pick vegetables from your garden in the cool of early morning, before the heat of the sun evaporates some of their moisture, and when the temperature of the plant is at its lowest. Both heat and lack of moisture accelerate food deterioration, so early-morning harvesting pays a double dividend: it prevents decay and enables food to maintain that vital quality of freshness for a longer period. If you soak your vegetables in order to restore their crispness, moisture on the outside surfaces can cause them to decay in storage. Some authorities claim that the best time to harvest a crop is in the evening, after the sun has been shining and the activity of the plant is the greatest. They claim this product to be nutritionally superior. We believe that our method is far more practical because an evening harvest means that the sun's heat remaining in the plant has yet to be dissipated.

The first pickings of any plant are the choicest in flavor and are nutritionally superior to subsequent pickings. The variations in flavor between the first and last pickings of certain fruits, particularly strawberries, confirm this. Studies have shown that the vitamin C content drops about 50 percent in the first two weeks of picking. The sweetness of sugar in the first strawberries is disguised by the tartness of the high ascorbic acid content. As more and more berries are produced, leaving less and less of the vitamin C in the plant, the sweetness of the flavor then predominates in later pickings. Those who prefer such later pickings of strawberries because of their increased sweetness do not realize that they have lost much of the important vitamin C. Such marked flavor differences confirm marked nutritional differences. Jam makers know the exceptional jelling quality of the first berries in contrast with that of later pickings. The latter often will not jell without the addition of pectin.

May—The Spring Harvest

The word "harvest" conjures up an autumnal scene complete with bare trees and a dusting of snow on the ground. In fact, on any organic farm, harvesting and planting are carried out throughout the growing season. Indeed, it is the fall planting of rhubarb and chive clumps that makes the earliest spring harvesting possible. The tenderness and flavor of these first crops not only add zest to the palate but also heighten anticipation of the harvests to come.

An early seeding of spinach and radishes with transplantings of onions, beets and lettuce guarantees continuing spring harvests. A word of warning to those who might be carried away by spring enthusiasm untempered by experience: make sure that the soil has dried enough to break up and become loose and soft before you work it, or your optimistic harvesting schedule will be seriously disrupted. Spinach illustrates the importance of early planting in well-drained soil. If spinach is planted later than March in our soil, the heat of summer produces tough, woody, seed-producing stalks rather than the tender leaves of spring-harvested spinach.

Leaf lettuce, another of our favorite early harvests, stands up to warm, damp weather much better than head lettuce, which tends to rot on the underside next to the soil. We prefer leaf lettuce at our table because of its uniform tenderness and because it is truly a green vegetable. The outside leaves of head lettuce are a beautiful green but are often tough, and the choice inside heart is not green enough to have the nutritional qualities of a true green vegetable.

Early June—Strawberries

People are not alone in enjoying the fruits of the harvest. At no time of the year were we more aware of this at Mylora than in early June when the strawberries, choicest of all fruits, began to ripen. Then we played host to early-morning gatherings of birds feasting before the berries were fully ripe. Some of the tactics we used in the battle of wits to save fruit included placing pans of fresh water in the fields for the birds, hoping to satisfy their thirst and to cut down on their wholesale consumption. Other organic growers have suggested planting, close to the cultivated crop, uncultivated fruit, such as a wild berry, that ripens at the same time to attract birds. The birds seem to prefer the wild, somewhat bitter taste of these wild berries to the comparatively bland flavor of the cultivated varieties preferred by humans. The birds' preference suggests that some of the nutritive qualities of our sophisticated and newer varieties have been lost, since wild creatures will always choose the most nutritious ones.

To enjoy the true, rich flavor of strawberries, you should pick and eat them immediately when they are thoroughly warmed by the sun.

Late June—Peas

Spring peas, freshly picked, are a favorite of epicures the world over. Many have vowed that heaven on earth could be attained by following the harvest of new potatoes, green peas and spring lamb around the world. Unfortunately, the increasing labor costs of picking peas by hand may soon cause the disappearance of fresh green peas in their pods from the stores, meaning that only those who grow their own will enjoy them in the future.

Peas should be picked when the pods are filled and before they begin to show any signs of lighter coloring along the edge of the pod. This fading of the pod's color happens at the same time as the peas harden and lose their sweetness. However, even at this stage they can still be enjoyed when cooked.

End of June—Beets, Lettuce and Green Onions

After peas come the delicious harvests of beets (from the first seeding), lettuce and green onions, all of which come to kitchen readiness at roughly the same time.

Early to Mid-July—Raspberries

Raspberries require picking every other day at first, but in extremely hot weather the accelerated ripening can make daily picking necessary. If the growing season has been dry, raspberries respond well to a generous watering at the beginning of the harvest. When harvesting is completed, all the canes that bore fruit should be cut down to the level of the soil surface.

Mid-July—Extra Planting

Since early harvesting leaves empty spaces in the garden, an immediate planting should be done to continue the process of soil building. If further vegetable planting for later harvesting is not practical in any one year, plant a cover crop to refurbish the soil and protect it. Otherwise, you might do what we sometimes did at Mylora—use empty spaces to grow more food for later harvesting. In fact, some crops grow well into the winter months. Broccoli that is seeded early in July usually produces medium to heavy yield. Even after the center head is harvested, the side shoots continue to grow and are just as palatable as the main head. In our climate, such shoots continue to develop until the winter becomes too severe. Lettuce, peas, beans, carrots and beets are other crops that can be seeded in spaces left by the early harvesting.

Mid-July—New Potatoes, Peas and Beans

About the time the raspberries are ripe and ready for picking, some tiny new potatoes can be stolen from the hills without damaging any growing potato plants. Put your hand carefully into the soft soil and feel gently for potatoes. Sneak just one or two small potatoes from each plant, disturbing the roots as little as possible.

New potatoes make for memorable dining. A true delicacy, they are highly perishable until the skin is hard and set, by which time they scarcely qualify as new potatoes. As long as the skin rubs off easily, new potatoes will not keep very long. Refrigerate to keep them from becoming soft. Even then any area where the skin is broken is vulnerable to invasion by disease organisms, which will eventually destroy the potato. The season is short, but the flavor is unique.

This phenomenon underlines a well-known but largely ignored fact about vegetable skins and the area immediately beneath them. In the human body the skin is the first protective line of defense, and when it is damaged you hurry and protect it against invading organisms. The skin of a potato protects the potato in the same way. If you damage the skin of a potato while it is still growing, it will heal as human skin heals, providing it is healthy, as will the skin of any living thing. The skin contains substances that protect the plant and its fruit for the benefit of the consumer. To remove and discard the skin with its valuable, disease-resisting layer of flesh is one of modern society's most wasteful acts.

Check your potatoes for scab, obvious rough patches on the skin. We were able to control scab on potatoes, which shows up at harvest time, by growing red clover for two years on our heavier soil before planting potatoes.

The harvesting of the second seeding of peas coincides with the raspberry picking. Because the weather will be hotter than during the first harvest, take care to pick peas in the cool part of the day. If this is not possible, cool the peas rapidly after picking. The sun's heat together with the heat the peas generate themselves when heaped in a container can affect quality and flavor in a matter of hours.

Yellow and green beans do not deteriorate as rapidly as peas and can wait an extra day or two between pickings during a busy season. They also do not generate as much heat, nor does the flavor change as readily as that of the sumptuous pea. Beans should be eaten when they are 4 to 5 inches (10 to 13 centimetres) long, but before the seeds inside have developed enough to show their positions in the pod.

End of July—Cucumbers and Zucchini

Cucumbers and zucchini should be ready for harvest next. In cucumbers, lighter coloring on the skin occurs when the cucumber is changing from growth to seed development, resulting in a loss of succulence. Flavor and crispness are best when the skin is dark green.

There are as many notions concerning the optimum length of a zucchini as there are possible lengths of the squash itself. Personally, I have found little to choose in flavor between a 6-inch (15-centimetre) and a 2-foot (60-centimetre) zucchini, so when you pick them is a personal choice. If you want young zucchini continuously throughout the summer, you must pick them as soon as they reach about 8 to 10 inches (20 to 25 centimetres) or the plant will stop producing new fruits and direct its energy into the production of seeds. If, however, a quantity is needed for winter storage, it is better to leave an entire bush unpicked until the late fall harvest. The small fruits from the remaining bushes should be picked frequently. For winter soil protection, rye can be seeded between the rows after the last cultivation.

Early August—Corn, Tomatoes and Cereal Grains

Corn—the long-awaited delicacy of late summer—is, like springtime peas, a perishable product. To reap the full flavor and abundant food value, eat corn as soon as possible after picking it. Removing the husks (the protective covering of the corn cobs) hours in advance of using the corn causes deterioration.

Corn can be picked when the kernels on the cob have developed fully all along its length to the tip. You can determine this by firmly squeezing the middle of the cob between the thumb and forefinger and running the pressure along to the tip. If the cob is fully formed right to the tip, open the tip of the husk and have a look at the kernels. If they have not yet filled out, cover them again with the husk and leave the cob on the stalk to mature further. When this test cob is ready for picking, take note of the dryness of the tassel silks at the tip of the cob and use this as a guide to judge which of the other cobs are ready to harvest. Do not open all the husks, because insects sometimes attack the corn kernels once the husks have been opened.

Corn requires far more heat than other grains for the seed to ripen. In our area, the cobs must be picked before the weather becomes too wet. We found we could not produce the hard corn kernels that keep well in storage.

Tomatoes begin to ripen when the corn is ready to harvest. As soon as the tomatoes start to ripen, the soil can be seeded with clover, which will grow through the winter. Tomatoes are best picked when fully ripe. If, however, frost threatens the plants, pick them as soon as they show some coloring and bring them inside to ripen. To ensure proper ripening, be certain that the temperature of the storage room does not drop below 50°F (10°C) or the tomatoes will decay rather than ripen. If tomatoes are left on the vine to ripen, watch for weather reports so that you can protect them against frost. If frost threatens, the plants can be covered with plastic or other material, or, if the area is large, it can be irrigated. If the temperature then drops to freezing point, ice will form and provide some protection to the plants.

Cereal grains, such as oats and wheat, ripen at about the same time as the first corn and tomatoes are being harvested. In small plantings, the stalks can be cut before the grain is fully ripe, tied in bundles and moved to a sheltered area where the final ripening can be completed. When the seed is completely ripe and dry, flail it on a threshing floor (a smooth, hard-surfaced floor), where very little is lost.

Early September—Winter Onions

Onions should be ready for harvesting early in September. Unlike other root vegetables, onions are never hilled up. If they are, the necks become thicker and the onions will not cure or dry satisfactorily and therefore will not keep. They should be pulled up when the tops have died and have begun to dry up. Leave the roots exposed on the soil surface through several fine days so that they will dry. At the time of harvesting onions for winter storage, the weather should be dry enough to be able to get the cultivating machine in, stir the soil and seed the winter crop.

If the weather is wet and the onions have to remain on the soil for more than 3 or 4 days, they should be turned over at least once after the weather has cleared up so that all surfaces have a chance to dry. When this is done, gather the onions into mesh sacks and place them where there is free air circulation. They must not be piled in a heap but arranged so that the air can circulate around them. To determine the dryness of stored onions, test them by moving them around by hand. If the onions rustle when moved, they are dry enough. A cool temperature is necessary to inhibit sprouting.

After onions are harvested, the area should be seeded heavily with rye. It is never a good idea to have a green manure crop growing while onions are in the field, since it makes it difficult to dry the onions sufficiently for satisfactory winter storage. This crop, therefore, must be followed by soil improvement crops, not another food crop.

Mid-September—Winter Potatoes

Before digging potatoes for winter storage, test some from different areas to be certain that the skins are firm and will not rub off with the pressure of your fingers. A delay of two or three weeks may be necessary to allow the potatoes to develop a firm enough skin and reach the optimum state to guarantee good keeping qualities. The drier the soil and the drier the digging weather, the longer and better the potatoes will keep in storage.

In our area, late potatoes cause damage to the soil. By the time the potatoes are harvested, it is far too late and wet to work the soil to seed anything else. It is better to plant potatoes with a shorter growing season so that a regular crop of rye can be grown in time to nourish and protect the soil.

As is mentioned earlier, late blight is a nagging worry to every potato farmer no matter how large or small an area is devoted to potatoes. The middle of August is the time to look for the first symptoms: small dead spots on the leaves. If a moist area is discernible around the dead spot when the leaf is held up to the light, the probability is that blight fungus is active and the crop is in jeopardy. If there is any evidence that these symptoms are spreading, speedy action is required. The tops of all the plants in the field must be cut off and allowed to dry up in order to halt any further spread of the disease. The cutting of the tops, if done early enough, prevents the infection from travelling down the stem into the roots and destroying the potatoes themselves. In areas drier than ours, where there is no danger of blight and no problem with excessive soil moisture at digging time, the potato tops can be left to die naturally.

Dry potatoes, therefore, are the first and most important requisite for good storage. Housed in complete darkness at a temperature of just under 40°F (4.4°C), the crop should provide prime eating fare through the winter. Too low a temperature causes changes that give the potatoes an unusually sweet flavor, whereas a high temperature causes the potatoes to dehydrate, soften and lose weight. We usually counted on keeping our Mylora crop in prime condition at atmospheric temperature until February. After this time, potatoes left in storage keep better under refrigeration because the lower temperature slows down the sprouting process.

Commercial growers use a chemical that inhibits the natural sprouting process. This chemical, along with numerous other artificial aids, may have unknown effects on consumers. These materials are labelled "safe" only because there is no proof yet that they have caused harm to humans.

Mid-October—Carrots, Beets, Parsnips and Turnips

Carrots and beets (from later seedings) for winter storage are harvested while the soil is quite wet so that they will remain firm and succulent for a long time. The Mylora choice of carrot variety—the Nantes—was based on its superb eating quality. Unfortunately, it has a tendency to split during harvesting if it is too full of moisture and unless it is handled very gently. One solution we tried successfully was to pull the carrots out of the soil and stand them up, stooked like grain, with leaves turned to the sun to extract some of the excess moisture and make them less brittle. The commercial trade favors a longer carrot with a tough inner core that bends rather than breaks, even when extra moisture is stored in it. Economically sound though this is, it is another example of how flavor, the very hallmark of quality, is considered a secondary factor.

Winter storage for carrots and beets is uncomplicated. Remove carrot tops right down to the carrot itself. Then pile them on well-drained ground under a 4-inch (10-centimetre) soil covering, which protects them from freezing. Should the winter prove very severe, extra soil can be added for additional protection. The pile can be as long as necessary but should not be wider than about 30 inches (75 centimetres) or higher than about 22 inches (55 centimetres). If the piles of carrots are wider or deeper, the heat the stored carrots generate cannot dissipate quickly enough and the temperature within the pile rises. The carrots then begin the second or seed-producing phase of their life, and nourishment from the carrot will go into the growing roots and the tops, which can't be eaten. Keeping this in mind, you must remove the additional soil covering that you applied during severe weather as soon as the danger of heavy frost is past.

Summer-planted carrots do not grow to a large size but when grown in a nourishing soil will be tender and can be left in the soil all winter. Such storage is feasible provided that an ample supply of this staple vegetable has been harvested from the main planting and is safely stored against unpredictable weather conditions. If you wish to enjoy carrots fresh from the garden all winter by leaving them in the soil, you must be prepared to lose all or some of them to heavy frost, unless you rush to cover them with a layer of straw when heavy frost threatens.

Beets differ from carrots; if the tops are dead and thoroughly dried, beets can be stored as they are. However, should the beets still have leaves growing, the leaves should be cut off half an inch (1 centimetre) above the beet. If the leaves are cut right down to the beet, the beet will bleed and some of the nutrients will be lost, as well as some of the attractive dark red color of the root. The beets can otherwise be stored the same way as the carrots.

Parsnips and turnips are also stored in the same way as carrots. Their flavor improves, however, if they have suffered a touch of frost before being harvested. If parsnips and turnips are planted in well-drained soil, they can be left in the ground and dug up as needed. Once the temperature stays below freezing, they can be covered with soil and will keep admirably. Storing these vegetables in boxes of sand in a cool place is also satisfactory.

End of October—Harvesting and Storing Crops

The end of October is also the end of harvesting crops for winter storage at Mylora. As the last of the plants are pulled, take care to leave behind the weeds still growing among them so that some covering remains to protect an otherwise bare and vulnerable soil. A dressing of hay, straw, manure or other organic material on the soil surface affords excellent winter protection. Crops from which only the seed is removed, such as cereals, peas and beans, leave more vegetation on the soil surface than root crops and consequently provide better protection for the soil.

Storing food effectively is as important as soil care, planting and harvesting in the farmer's scale of priorities. This means removing heat and moisture to slow down the life process of food so that it can be consumed in its living state. One of the basic principles of organic farming, as laid down by Sir Albert Howard, is that living people need living food. Harvested food is still alive and should remain alive if it is to provide the best nourishment.

Refrigeration

Vegetables that are to be eaten soon after harvesting should be kept in the refrigerator until they are prepared for the table.

Washed vegetables do not keep as long as unwashed vegetables, so do not wash your vegetables before storing them. Just before preparing them for the table, wash them in cold water. Once the preparation of vegetables has begun and any surfaces have been exposed by cutting, they must be protected from contact with the air, so wrap, cover with a liquid or seal in containers to prevent further oxidation, which will diminish their appearance, nutrition and flavor. Cold air blowing on the vegetables will dehydrate and wilt them. Therefore, coil-type refrigerators, which do not depend on air circulation, are preferable for storing vegetables.

The ideal refrigeration temperature for most hardy types of vegetables is about 34°F (1°C), so try to get as close to this point as possible to give them a longer life. Potatoes, however, should be kept at about 40°F

(4.4°C). Many vegetables freeze at temperatures just slightly lower than 32°F (0°C).

Freezing

Freshness is a prime consideration when vegetables are to be canned or frozen. As living organisms, they require diligent care and attention. Low temperature and high moisture content must be maintained until they have been preserved or otherwise protected against deterioration. Food must be frozen rapidly. Smaller packages freeze much faster than larger sizes.

To prepare corn for freezing, drop the cobs in boiling water for six to eight minutes and then remove the kernels from the cob by cutting with a sharp knife from the stem down. Pack the kernels in plastic bags and place in the freezer. Without the cobs, extra space is available in the freezer for additional food.

If you intend to freeze strawberries from your own organic garden, pick them carefully. If they are dusty and have to be washed, be sure to leave the hulls on the berries until after washing. Otherwise, the hole left by the core will fill with water, which will be difficult to remove. Raspberries can be packed directly into the freezer carton after picking.

Small, sun-ripened tomatoes can be frozen whole. Wash them if necessary, but be sure to dry them thoroughly, then put them in bags for freezing. During the long winter months they add fresh flavor to stews, soups and casseroles.

Harvesting and Storing Herbs

For winter storage, spring-seeded herbs must be gathered just when the plants are fully developed but before they start to ripen. When well dried, they should be tied in small bunches and hung, heads downward, in a dry, airy room away from the light. Leaves and seeds should be ground just before using; otherwise they rapidly lose their piquancy. Fresh herbs can be stored in airtight containers in the refrigerator. For gourmet cooking, nothing replaces herbs fresh from the garden.

Chapter Ten
Sprouting

There is nothing quite so new as something old rediscovered.

Anonymous

Sprouting is the beginning of the life cycle of a seed, an integral part of nature's provision to ensure perpetuation of the species. As seeds sprout, nutritional changes occur. Sprouting augments the content of vitamins, amino acids, carbohydrates and other nutrients. This extra nutrition in sprouts is akin to the unique composition of colostrum, the first mother's milk produced for a newborn baby, and to the nutrition provided by royal jelly, a special food that helps transform a newly hatched worker bee into a queen bee, thus ensuring the life of the next generation. In the same way, the sprouting seed, enriched by nature to start its new life, provides the seedling with the ultimate in nutrition.

A seed is composed of a tiny living germ complete with a genetic pattern. Surrounding and protecting that germ is a plentiful food supply adequate to energize the new life from the time germination begins until the shoot breaks through the soil. Enclosing the germ and its food supply is an outer casing (in grains, this casing is called the bran). The casing jealously guards its tiny, living treasure, protecting it from adverse conditions. Its covering resists moisture until the temperature, moisture and light required for continuing growth are appropriate.

Sprouts, the most nutritionally superior, inexpensive, easy-to-grow food that exists, are especially good for growing children and make an ideal home crop. Sprouted grains, for example, contain large amounts of vital nutrients. Wheat is the most available and least expensive of all.

Two Stories

The following incident was told to me by an elderly woman, who had heard it from her grandfather. In World War I, when the Germans and Russians were fighting in rye fields in the middle of winter, often the only food available was the rye seed, which had been harvested and stood in piles in the fields. A large pile of cereal seed will not burn, even with the "scorched earth" policy of those days. Strangely, the Russians seemed to be in much better physical condition than the Germans, even though both were subsisting on rye seed—what was the explanation? It was a mystery to the Germans.

This mystery was solved when the Germans, needing additional warm clothing, took it from the bodies of dead Russian soldiers. They discovered that the Russian soldiers carried small canvas bags into which they put wet rye seed. The soldiers carried these bags under their clothing next their skin, where the heat of their bodies germinated the seed. After a couple of days, they had an excellent source of nutrition in the form of sprouted grain—palatable, soft, sweet and easy to chew. The sprouted seed also provided bulk. The German soldiers had only the hard, cold seed, which required good teeth to chew or else it would be indigestible.

Here was one novel method of sprouting—preparing the food while fighting the enemy! It was simple, easy and free of costly or bulky equipment.

Another incident shows how resourceful some people can be. It has been reported that Captain Cook insisted that the beer that was brewed aboard his ship be made from sprouted grain. The result was that the sailors did not suffer from scurvy—a condition caused by a lack of vitamin C. I imagine that sometimes the grain got too wet to be used for baking and started to sprout, and that instead of discarding it, Cook decided to use it to make the beer. He was possibly driven to do this when the normal supply of food that provides the vitamin C was almost exhausted, as would occur on extraordinarily long voyages.

Sprouts: The Ultimate Food

Much energy is required to send hungry rootlets foraging through the warm, moist soil in search of food. Still more energy is required by the seed to thrust its tiny leaf shoot through the surface of the soil so that it can receive the rays of the sun to energize its growth. All of this seems an extraordinarily large amount of energy for such a tiny seed to expend. Where did it all come from?

Every farmer knows that if certain soils containing much clay have been subjected to heavy rain followed by hot sun, the surface is baked hard and the sown seed may not be able to penetrate this crust. Under such circumstances a germinating seed attempts its upward thrust to the light, but being unable to penetrate the crust it changes to a lateral thrust, still seeking a soft spot to go upward toward the light. Thrusting upwards to the right or left, it searches for an exit from the dark soil. A seedling such as this looks more like a corkscrew than a straight vertical shoot. It continues its upward thrust, now forced to travel laterally as long as its considerable energy lasts. But where does this prodigious energy come from—the energy that would start the growth of a small plant or even a huge tree, destined to grow for hundreds of years?

Thinking about it more and more, I wondered if, in the process of germination, the flour surrounding the tiny germ of life changes within that short period of time from carbohydrate to something extra special, something to give that tiny seedling the strength to reach up and receive energy from the sun. As an organic farmer, I thought this was a logical expectation, since, as we have already seen, nature is extremely provident in catering to new life.

After much searching through copies of the *Journal of Food Science,* I discovered that such a thing actually does occur. Essential nutrients do increase during germination—some a little, others a lot. Here we have an increase in vital food components—supernutrition for the taking. What a blessing for those in real need!

Of course, sprouting has been known and used for centuries in China and India. Alfalfa and bean sprouts have also been on the shelves of our markets for many years, sold as green vegetables. Those used as green vegetables have been allowed to sprout further than those I am advocating, so their concentration of nutrients has been diluted throughout the larger plant mass. I advocate consuming sprouts at a much earlier stage of growth, when the big nutrient increase occurs within the seed capsule. The sprouts are ready in two to three days but can even be eaten a little earlier.

World Hunger: A Solution

While I worked growing food for Canadians, I often thought about the tragedy of world hunger; it occurred to me that sprouting would be a solution to the problem of supplying fresh, highly nutritious food to people in developing countries. Sprouting seeds could conceivably provide a practical solution to an immense world problem. Sprouting is a simple, low-cost project that anyone can undertake anywhere, with minimal equipment, to obtain a nutritional bonanza.

For people in developing countries, sprouting provides a welcome variety in diet, involving a change from simple cereal to its fresh vegetable counterpart, and, visually, from brown food to green. Experiments showing the benefits of sprouting were conducted at the Tanzania Food-Nutrition Centre at Dar es Salaam under the direction of Dr. Wilbald Lorri, as well as at Maharaja University in Baroda, India, under the direction of Dr. Chinnamma John. In Dr. John's experiments, children whose diets of gruel were fortified with flour composed of 5 percent ground, sprouted grain grew more rapidly, put on more weight and were ill for fewer days than children whose diets did not include this flour. Dr. John, now Dr. (Sr.) Serena, has also found that sprouting provides an excellent source of nutrition for tube-fed babies with chronic diarrhea or other intestinal problems, surgical patients who cannot eat by mouth, elderly persons who have a very full feeling with their regular meals and might not receive sufficient nutrients, and pregnant women who also suffer from this full feeling.

Another benefit of sprouting is the sprouts' chlorophyl content. The chlorophyl in wheat sprouts has been found to inhibit the mutagenic (mutation-causing) effects of carcinogens.

Dr. P.L. Finney, an agricultural researcher at Ohio State University, has spent many years researching the subject of sprouting and its effects on human nutrition. He has not found one report of adverse effects resulting from germination. His research results varied from very positive to positive, but none were negative.

The most common basic food given to starving people is the seed of the cereal plants—plants that belong to the grass family. Many cereals, such as wheat, oats, barley, rice, sorghum and corn, are used for human consumption. The seeds of these cereals are concentrated, stable foods. In the developed world, they are grown in large quantities using highly mechanized equipment and usually yield a surplus for export.

Most edible seeds can be sprouted. Legumes such as alfalfa and various types of beans are also used for sprouts in North America.

Sprouting organically grown seeds will give you the ultimate food. However, if organic seeds are not available, sprouting commercial seeds will still provide you with supernutrition. One does not even have to acquire a taste for sprouts, since they are bland and can easily be eaten alone or incorporated into a wide variety of everyday dishes.

Keep in mind that the principles of sprouting are constant, but the techniques may vary slightly depending on the kind of seed used. Experiment with the seeds that are available to you, keeping in mind the factors basic to the behavior of germinating seeds: temperature, light, moisture and the age, size and hardness of the seed.

The Sprouting Process

Seeds are dormant living entities. In order to make them sprout, you must provide the right conditions of warmth and moisture to begin the first stage in their life cycle. On the first day of this cycle, seeds become lighter in color and swell. On the second day, threadlike growths emerge, indicating the start of the sprouting process. In about 48 to 72 hours at 70°F (21°C) or more, the sprouts are ready for consumption.

As the seedling develops, it grows more roots, stalks and leaves; because it increases in bulk, the vital nutrients become less concentrated. The tiny sprout is a sweeter, far more nutritious food than the larger sprout; be sure to capture this richness at its prime.

How to Sprout for Household Quantities

Sprouting can be done in your kitchen at room temperature, without soil, with little equipment or effort. You can sprout grains and legumes. The following are examples: wheat, alfalfa, soybeans, garbanzo beans, lentils, navy beans, peas. An additional benefit of sprouting legumes is that they are easier to digest sprouted than unsprouted.

Materials
    viable, edible seed
    a large, clean glass jar
    clean cheesecloth, coarse cloth, or nylon mesh and rubber band or

string, or sprouting lid (plastic screen sprouting lids are available in most health food stores)

Procedure
1. Fill 1/3 of the jar with viable, edible seeds.
2. Fill jar with water and wash seeds by rinsing a few times.
3. Remove floating pieces of seed, and drain water.
4. Add fresh water to 3/4 full.
5. Soak 4 to 6 hours at room temperature. Soybeans require 12 to 16 hours of soaking. Do not soak too long or the water may become cloudy, which is an indication of nutrient loss.
6. If you do not have a lid and are using cheesecloth or mesh, place it over the mouth of the jar and secure it with a rubber band or string. Set the jar on a sharp angle to drain for 4 to 8 hours.
7. Rinse thoroughly and drain again. Do this every 4 to 8 hours for 1 to 3 days, or until the sprouted part grows to approximately the length of the seed. Between rinsings, ensure that the jar maintains a sharp angle so that all the residual water will drain out of the jar, but do not make it airtight. Any water remaining on the sprouts will cause decay, and an unpleasant sour smell will result.

Sprouts will be ready to eat in about 48 hours if room temperature is over 70°F (21°C); if the temperature is cooler, they will take a little longer. The sprouts will be soft, chewy and slightly sweet when they are ready.

Beginning of soaking in jar of water.

Sprouts ready to eat. Sprouted part approximately the length of seed.

A bowl of sprouts ready to eat.

Sprouting Large Quantities

Method 1

Materials

For experimental purposes, I used a piece of plywood about 18 inches by 36 inches (46 centimetres by 91 centimetres) with a lip 2 inches (5 centimetres) high along the two long sides and one short side. However, any flat surface with a slight slope for drainage will do.

You will need about 20 pounds (9 kilograms) of seed.

Procedure

1. After thoroughly rinsing the seeds, soak them for 4-8 hours in a pail or vessel that will hold three times as much water as the seed to be sprouted, then drain.
2. Rinse the seeds again, although this is not essential if there is a water shortage.
3. Place the seeds from the container on the surface of the board,

allowing the seeds to drain by leaving the board tilted slightly downward.
4. Add enough water two or three times a day to keep the mass of seeds just moist.
5. Mix or stir the mass after adding water to ensure even germination; otherwise, the center of the mass will develop considerable heat and grow more rapidly than the outer seeds. Mixing or stirring also ensures adequate aeration to prevent mildew, objectionable organisms and undesirable odor.

Method 2
Materials and Procedure
You can use hessian sacking instead of a board. Just remember to keep the seeds moist yet drained and keep them stirred to ensure aeration. The sack can be hung up or remain resting on a flat surface and moved several times a day to maintain even moisture and temperature throughout the mass of seeds. This method will slow down the germination considerably, since the evaporation of the moisture from the sack will have a marked cooling effect.

Using Your Sprouts

Sprouts are best eaten fresh, but they will keep in the refrigerator for a few days. You can use them in many ways. Most sprouts, except soybean sprouts, can be eaten raw. Add sprouts to stews, soups and salads, or use them mixed with peanut butter or cream cheese to spread on sandwiches. Some sprouts can be used whole in baking, mixed with nuts and served as snacks, or mixed with fruit, honey and peanut butter to form a soft candy. You can stir-fry sprouts with herbs, curry, onions and other ingredients of your choice. Soybean sprouts, steamed for five minutes, make an excellent meat substitute.

If you cannot use sprouts fresh, they should be thoroughly dried out for later use. Place a thin layer on a tray to be dried in the air. Drying in the oven heat could damage the nutrients. Stir sprouts two or three times per day. When they are thoroughly dry, they will keep a long time. Freezing sprouts is not recommended.

The garbanzo bean, also called the chickpea, is worthy of special note. Since it is a legume, it is particularly rich in protein. Furthermore, sprouting more than doubles the amount of protein in the legume. Garbanzo beans can be eaten after 12 hours of sprouting time or even sooner, but they are better after 24 hours of sprouting and possibly attain their high protein content at about 48 hours. They are delectable raw as a snack once you have come to appreciate the flavor. They are the size of a small cherry, and it is difficult to sit at the table when they are on a plate and not keep nibbling on them.

If you have a grinder, you can grind your own flour from your dried wheat sprouts. Not only will you have the increased nutrition resulting from the sprouts, but you will also have the entire wheat grain. The manufacturers will not have had the opportunity to steal either the highly nutritious wheat germ or the all-important bran. This flour will keep well, and because it is bland it can be easily introduced into the regular cooking schedule. In Tanzania flour from sprouted grain is called "power flour"; in India, it is called A.R.F., or amylase rich food. In these places, mothers sprout and prepare gruel with power flour for their children.

Remember that sprouting deals with living, growing, and vulnerable seeds. Care must be taken not to introduce any unnatural factors such as extra heat to expedite the process.

Chapter Eleven
Life Beyond the Farm

The final crop of any land is people
—and the spirit of the people.

Robert Flaherty

Long before I began writing this book, a freeway was built through the center of our farm. The two parts of the farm were connected only by main roads and a freeway overpass. The shortest distance between each part was approximately 2 miles (3 kilometres), making the return road trip 4 miles (6 kilometres). On a busy day, we had to make many such trips. The increasing traffic from a new subdivision nearby exaggerated the time and distance involved in picking up a small load of vegetables or merely checking on operations. The trip also involved the danger of merging our slow-moving farm vehicles with speeding traffic coming from the freeway. It was particularly dangerous moving long irrigation pipes with a tractor and wagon, which took more time than one traffic light would allow to make a left-hand turn and clear the intersection.

We also recognized the danger of the lead emissions from automobile exhaust; at the time, unleaded gasoline was not yet in general use. The drifting lead fumes posed a serious threat since they would pollute both the crops in the fields and the soil itself for years to come. We felt very uncertain and insecure about a future we could not begin to predict.

A few years later, further difficulty arose. In our area, most of the sales of root vegetables were controlled by the local marketing board. The board had been good enough to give us permission to sell our vegetables directly to a large chain of department stores as well as to health food stores. This privilege meant that our organically grown vegetables did not have to go into the general pool of ordinary commercially grown vegetables. In this way, we were able to maintain our identity. We also obtained from these stores the premium price necessary to cover our higher growing costs, since hand and mechanical weeding is far more expensive than using herbicide sprays. After a number of years, the marketing board wanted to set standards for organic produce, which in itself was not a bad idea.

The board reasoned that other growers who might choose to grow food organically would expect the same privileges that we had had. However, there were as yet no standards anywhere in Canada to determine what constituted organic produce. Until acceptable standards were put in place, we were no longer permitted to enjoy the privilege of marketing our produce directly and separately.

These very disturbing factors worried us. Should we sell our farm and move to another area? We decided that to set up a new organic farm was out of the question. Since continuing with our existing farm was becoming impossible, we decided to retire from farming.

One of the most pleasant aspects of our new way of life is that we are able to live in our home of fifty years. It is still surrounded by beautiful trees—truly the lungs of the earth—and our flower beds are colorful and eye-catching. However, we miss the pleasure of looking at straight rows of vigorous, weed-free vegetables.

We enjoy the many birds who find safe haven and nesting places in the trees and bushes we have planted. The lakes nearby provide fish for kingfishers and herons, and in spring the birches are full of a variety of birds.

Now that we have more time to watch God's creatures, we have bird feeders around our small patio and waterfall. This is my wife's domain: she feeds the birds and enjoys their battles over the choice tidbits. Sometimes we have our own small discussion over who gets the balance of the wheat when the sack is almost empty—Marian for her bird feeders, or me for my sprouting. Most often I am the one who goes to the store.

The little birds are Marian's favorites—she feeds them their special seeds. There are blackbirds with beautiful colors under their wings that can only be seen when they are in flight. We have a lovely old chestnut tree overhanging the patio, and the little birds perch on the branches waiting to be fed. If they don't get enough, they call for more, while the finches sing merrily after Marian feeds them. There are also chickadees, Cooper's hawks and marsh hawks, and other birds too numerous to mention.

Flocks of tame ducks live near our house, and we often see the eagles soaring overhead looking for prey. The pigeons who used to steal our green peas just as they were emerging from the soil are still with us, but we view them differently now. A few Canada geese also drop in occasionally.

A beautiful white owl used to overwinter in the barn. Pheasants take cover in the bushes from the hunters' guns. I still wait, always expecting the cock pheasant to finish up his "cock-a-doodle-do" just as the rooster does, but since he is a pheasant and not a rooster, he stops short at "cock-a-" and I feel I should finish it for him every time I hear it.

Each year since the patio was built, a duck has been visiting us in the spring looking for the wheat it remembers from the last year. Mr. Drake comes with his mate, and they do some of their courting on our patio. The drake would put many men to shame! He politely waits and watches while she eats; he is most attentive. He watches her get safely into the pool, and when she has satisfied her thirst, she clambers out and then they both fly away together. He does not eat, even though there is an abundant supply of food. This procedure soon stops, and finally, one day, she arrives on the patio trailing her ten pretty yellow ducklings—proud as anything to show them off! They all obey her as she leads them around the garden and eventually to the little pool when they are big enough. She watches them very closely and, at the slightest disturbance, calls them together and leads them—waddling in single file behind her—to her safe shelter in the bushes, well hidden from any predators. We watch them growing and fighting for food until their visits become more irregular and at last there is one final visit when they seem to say au revoir.

We have animals too. We do not often see the muskrat, but we hear the plop in the water at our approach. We appreciate the muskrats' work in helping to keep some of our drainage pipes clear. We also have a beaver who fells the poplar trees. We don't mind since poplars grow quickly and soon provide shade.

Most important, we continue to enjoy our home, where we are able to see what we value most—nature in all its beauty. By working hand in hand with nature, we have made a wonderful life. We have learned much, and we have had the privilege and pleasure of sharing it with others. We could not wish for more.

Finale

At the end of the twentieth century, we seem to place all our faith in new technological developments, looking with wonder and awe at the marvelous things that scientists are doing. We expect scientists to be able to correct everything that goes wrong, but we overlook the fact that in nature, such difficulties are merely symptoms of a deeper problem. We should be trying to remove the cause of the problem, not just fix the symptoms. When scientific developments merely fix the symptoms, other symptoms will continually appear as long as the cause remains.

We should also realize that in time, nature will solve its own problems. Our primary task is to support nature in maintaining itself. Nowhere is this more important than in caring for the soil, the very foundation of life on this earth. We must never forget that the important factor in soil fertility is the life present in the soil, the organisms that convert waste materials into ideal food for plants, upon which all life depends.

For skeptics who question the importance of microbial life in the soil, I present this metaphor: Think of the soil as a bank account given to us as a birthright. If we do not operate this account according to nature's rules, which must be learned by observation, our children will inherit a bankrupt account.

We sow seeds in the soil and then care for the plants as they grow. When they are mature, we harvest them and take with the harvest some of the capital fertility of the soil. In nature, after the crop is produced, some form of animal life consumes it and via its droppings returns the residue of the crop to the soil. If the crop is not consumed by animals, the leaves, fruit and seeds fall to the soil. This accumulation steadily enriches the soil—nothing is disturbed, and nothing is taken away. The capital remains intact. To this capital, interest is added each year in the form of an increase in leaves, fruit, seeds and so on. Such is the pattern nature provides, and it is the pattern we must follow.

The multitude of plants spread over the face of the earth have all adapted to their own particular environment. Throughout the centuries, life has changed and adapted, and through endless cycles plant materials have continued to enrich the soil. We must plan our agriculture in a way that is consistent with such natural cycles, keeping in mind that there are really only two important assets that we can hand down to our children—knowledge and a fertile soil. If we continue to damage and destroy our environment, to damage and destroy our soil, it is our children who will pay the price.

Environmentalists must direct their major efforts to protect our soil—the very basis of our health and the source of life. In order to protect the soil, not only must we stop the use of chemicals in agriculture but we must seriously limit them for other uses unless they can be completely recovered and recycled. To be able to grow without chemicals, we must change from chemical to organic or natural agricultural methods. Only then will we be saved from chemicals.

It is my hope that everyone, but particularly the younger generation, will try to discover the whole truth about the production of food. All too often, growing methods and materials used in agriculture are not disclosed, nor are accidental injuries to workers resulting from the use of chemicals made public. We must all work toward nutritionally good food, free from foreign substances, for everyone. Good health is a God-given birthright. Let's fight to keep it.

Index